On the Road to Angkor

On the Road to Angkor

Margret Hargreaves-Allen

iUniverse, Inc.
New York Lincoln Shanghai

On the Road to Angkor

Copyright © 2007 by Margret Hargreaves-Allen

iUniverse books may be ordered through booksellers or by contacting:

iUniverse
2021 Pine Lake Road, Suite 100
Lincoln, NE 68512
www.iuniverse.com
1-800-Authors (1-800-288-4677)

ISBN-13: 978-0-595-42654-6 (pbk)
ISBN-13: 978-0-595-86982-4 (ebk)
ISBN-10: 0-595-42654-9 (pbk)
ISBN-10: 0-595-86982-3 (ebk)

Printed in the United States of America

Dedicated to

Teddy and Manuela

Bamiyan
Indus
Taxila
Pakistan
Tibet
China
Yangtze
Taiwan
Brahmaputra
Bhutan
India
Mumbai
(Bombay)
Ajanta
Ellora
Hong Kong
Laos
Myanmar
(Burma)
Sukhothai
Siam
Bangkok
Angkor
Cambodia
Vietnam
Pacific
Ocean
Anuradhapura
Sigiriya
Polonnaruwa
Sri Lanka
(Ceylon)
Malaysia
Singapore
Indonesia
Indian Ocean
Borobodur
Bali
Java
Besakih

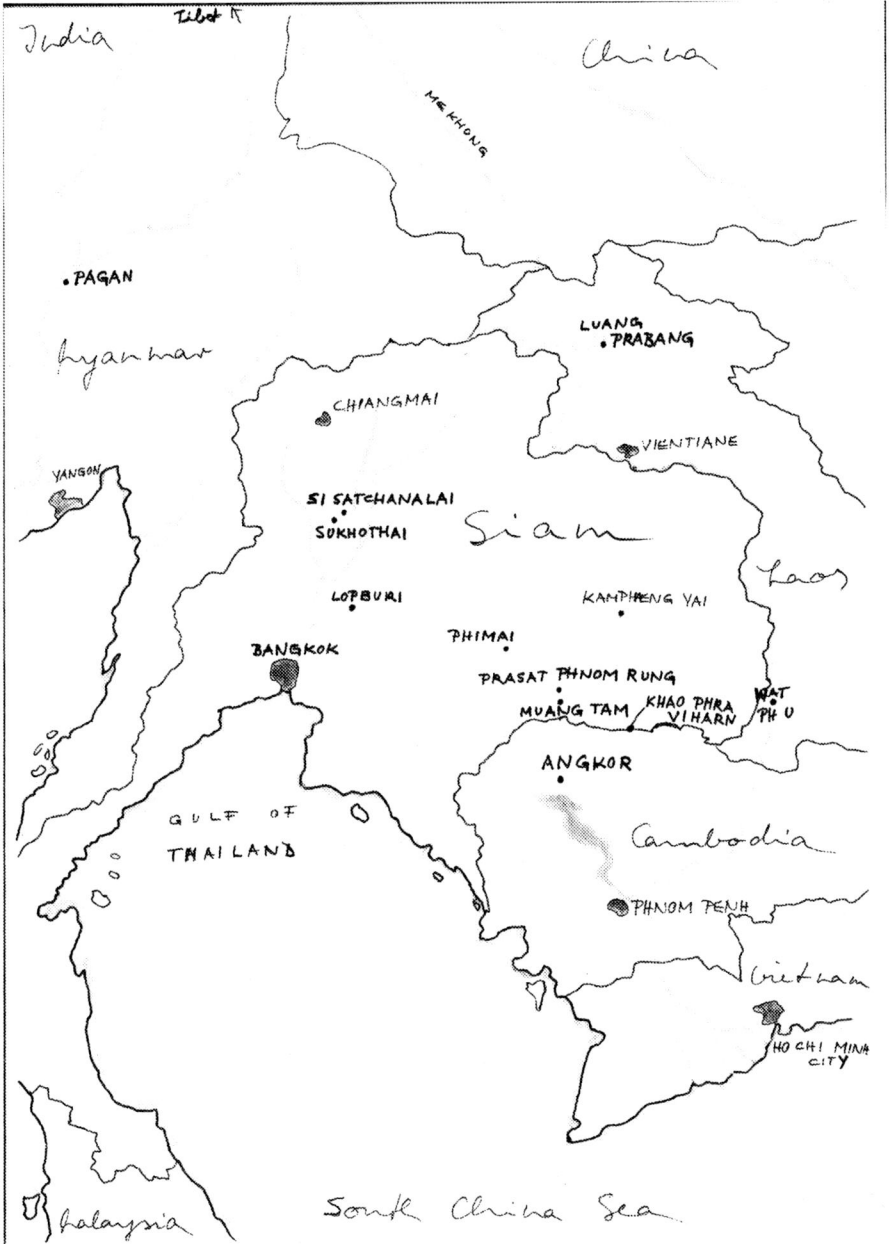

I started on the road to Angkor a long, long time ago and still I wanted to go there. And now I am, finally.

Maybe it started with "Siddhartha", Hermann Hesse's book, which I must have come across in a bookshop; then, when I had so much time. I read it, swallowed it, suspecting myself slightly of being duped—since its re-emergence had come as a result of a cult. Yet, while not wanting to be drawn into it, I was attracted by the cult.

I surprised myself when, touched by the outpourings of another's devotion, I started reading the book to a man who had hardly ever been exposed to literature, much less seen its link to his own existence. And just when I was beginning to think that I myself had been misled, he asked for more of Siddhartha.

And then I forgot about it. Or thought I had forgotten. For years.

And every time I mentioned my desire to go to Angkor, I was told firmly, by those who know, that "now is not a good time to go; there is fighting". Which in retrospect was an understatement.

But now, many, many years later, I was determined, and Angkor was reputed to be "open". So, the plan was to start on the "Royal Way", the long route of Khmer temples leading from the middle of present day Thailand all the way to Angkor, which in the days of walking or elephant travel was a journey of about twelve days. I had seen some of these temples before, long before any concerted attempts at restoration, in the years when I lived in Thailand towards the end of, and after, the Vietnam War; the time of the shadowy involvement of Cambodia, and the fall of Phnom

Penh. A new-found Thai friend, who had further stirred my interest by reading us excerpts on specific temples from Nagel's guide book of Thailand, sealed my motivation. It occurred to me to ask this very friend and his Italian wife if they would like to come along now, and they took over preparations from then on; with alacrity. An initial enquiring phone call, followed by many faxes. The inspiring news of a newly opened temple on the Thai/Cambodian border, Khao Phra Viharn, confirmed by a newspaper article, further excited us.

Malaria prophylaxis had to be started, and the Lariam started working on me. My companion from Harvard was crisp with me when I doubted the need for the drug; he coolly stated that 10% of the Khmer Rouge had died from malaria. So I started it as advised, a week before leaving, and, apart from a mild general restlessness and less desire for sleep, nothing much happened. Rather like jet lag.

The next thing that happened was that I missed my plane. It sounds rather unimportant in retrospect, but at the time, like a bad omen almost, I thought I had lost control of my mental faculties.

After the long period of anticipation I was sitting at my desk, having just given a cup of coffee to some friends from Austria. I was looking at my ticket with the thought of how well-organized everything was, when it struck me that the time mentioned on it was 10.30—no a.m. or p.m., as is done in America. There had been much talk with my travel agent of planes leaving late at night on the return journey, and I had automatically assumed it to be an evening flight. No doubt the Lariam was already working on my brain. In the end I did take an evening flight, and it was wonderfully empty.

And I arrived in Bangkok in the afternoon to a new net of flyovers, which enabled us to reach the Oriental in not much more than half an hour. Apparently, the Asian Games were about to start, an event that had spurred construction.

Asian Games. No-one had even heard of such things in England, and I am sure not in Continental Europe either. A new Asia, united in purpose and giving a much firmer, greater impression of natural self-importance. Although I consider myself a—hopefully—honourable South-East Asian, there was a shift in thought to be accommodated as a non-Asian, a re-arranging of one's own place in the order of things, however sympathetic one might be.

But the exquisitely polite welcome from the hotel's organizer at the airport, who even remembered me from previous stays, soon relaxed the initial shock of alienation. One sinks easily into the kindness of the Thais, and one is reminded that it is a country with a long Buddhist past, a country in which, although it has become a very modern nation indeed, Buddhism is still practiced today. I lived here once, spending much time outside, amongst comforting expanses of coarse grass and lazy old trees in whose branches hybrid orchids nestled, with a lotus pond to contemplate, easily forgetting the ferocious churn of Bangkok street life beyond, well protected by devoted lookers-after and a fierce Brittany spaniel. For the sake of the truth it must be recorded that eventually we too had to have a night watchman, but he was mostly asleep, which was considered quite normal. Night watchmen need to be well-paid so they in turn can pay off potential burglars. Sleep can then embrace all.

That was—

But—oh—what a reminder of the 20th century this city has become, with now idle construction cranes next to half-finished high rises, skeletons of no windows but huge height against a background of more high rises, diced about, amongst the old Chinese shop houses, the residences, temples, restaurants, bars. There are bars in other cities too but, if one believes Paul Theroux in *The Great Railway Bazaar* or Michel Houellebecq in *Plateforme*, Bangkok's are the apex of evil. Well, one finds what one looks for.

So, Bangkok must be left behind.

But not before seeing Mark again. He had been a friend when I had lived here, and after. He was often argumentative and quite impossible but always big spirited, fascinating because of his fearless experiences in South-East Asia. He had come down from the country that day to be with his old friends and me. To drag him away from his hideout in the wilderness of Khao Yai, a nature reserve where he had a house and where he was writing books about animals and jungle plants, was increasingly difficult; so I was told. And then there was the film he had made, also, when he was still a businessman. He showed it to us then, 1973 or 4 it must have been, having made it some years before. Of course, I had heard about Angkor Wat, seen photographs of the unison of trees and temples, but when I saw the film he had made, it dawned on me that one might actually be able to go there. So I questioned others about it and was firmly told not to go because of "the fighting"; told in a tone of voice censorious of the frivolous lust for adventure, in contempt of curiosity, at a time of war—real war.

The Vietnam War came to an end, but still the fighting continued in Cambodia. Horrendous stories circulated, stories about the fates of the temples and the monks, stories of Buddhism's being desecrated, mutilated, if not by landmines then by the forces of physical and mental destruction.

The night I saw Mark was just before I was finally going to Angkor. I exulted in rediscovering a friend I had assumed estranged for quite a few years—despite the laughter we had shared, and my fascination at hearing him talk. He knew everything about everything, but, as someone said, what he knew most about he never talked about. An Anglo-Scot with a great love of Italy, he had much in common with the spirited Victorian travelers, and he had landed in Thailand piloted by his love life, at an age of barely more than twenty. Eventually love had deserted him, I knew, but his spirit had grown, I now realized. He was still the same person, only more so, with a less vainglorious but more pragmatic, humane direction, as his subjects of conversation and his interpretation of these subjects showed. How strange that I should have been so very touched by his presence that night. When I had no foreboding of the drama to come.

Skyline of the Bangkok emerging now, with the richly adorned roofs of old Chinese buildings seen in front of a Buddhist temple, plus the high-rises introducing a note of the sobering life of today.

The next day my Harvard friend and I flew to Siem Reap, in Cambodia, a small town next to the ruins of Angkor. Our arrival was chilling. We were separated by armed guards the moment we entered the arrival hall: a basic shed of concrete, discoloured by humidity, as so often seen in Asia.

I felt very much on my own. Harvard vanished amongst uniforms reinforced by metal tags. Visions of Khmer Rouge suppression could not be suppressed. We were not held at gunpoint, but there was nonetheless an underlying threat of violence. By officials who felt that they were doing one altogether far too great a favour by granting one a $20 visa, and who expected one to kowtow to them and tolerate their aggressive, arrogant manner, no doubt from years of training to frighten people into doing what they wanted them to. Irritatingly, some of the people who trickled off the plane were prepared to appear meek for this purpose.

The Grand Hotel d'Angkor, where visitors "to the ruins" were taken in the thirties, was where we were to stay. The building looked before-the-turn-of-the-century-Colonial. But, of course, European architectural styles were re-enacted in Asia about fifty years after their creation. I had once lived in an old Colonial house which felt very much a part of the 19th century, only to find out that it had been built around the same time as this hotel, 1932.

Flopping, exhausted, onto the bed, looking forward to some tea served with the superb local limes, the first thing that struck me was the beauty of the silks which covered various pieces of furniture. On the tray were perfectly baked cookies. At least one thing Europeans have done well to pass on to Asians—all over Thailand and even in Singapore these baking traditions blend in so well with the local ones, kept alive by the local people by choice, not necessity.

But the road to Angkor only ended here. It started in Thailand, under the guidance of the Thai-Italian connection, as we called my friends Spha and Manuela—he a Thai national, she Italian but by now an honorary Thai. We went with them in their car: sobering 20th century motorways to start with, for what seemed like a very long time. But once off the main artery, snaking up towards the Khao Yai National Park, and then through a cattle-rearing area, we drove past clusters, if not plantations, of orchids. Huge old mango trees hinted at harvests of fruit rich beyond necessity, an abundance first suspected, then obvious. In the fields in between, we see diligent-looking water buffaloes, moving obediently but at their own pace, their young following closely behind.

Phimai was the first temple in the Thai North East that we were to visit. I had been to the site at a time when restoration had been started only tentatively and was made almost impossible by lack of funds. Those trying to do it—and I feared their idealism might be wasted—were paying their own expenses. They were young Thai archeologists from the Fine Arts Department in Bangkok; I was deeply moved by the dedication and humility, the great dignity with which they approached the excavations. The search for detail was painstaking. What a delight to see the Sanctuary again, with its monastic buildings, its moat and temple fully restored. Now one could grasp the architectural layout as it must have been at the beginning. There are those who say that the temples are more evocative in their unspoiled state, with trees growing through them, drowned in vegetation, and there are certain temples of which that is undoubtedly true—but to try and understand the genius of it all, must we not also know what they might have looked like when freshly built? Because in their linear purity and unity these were magnificent constructions.

Now that Phimai has been restored, one gains a clearer image of the life that it must have engendered, of the ideas that spurred the builders on to create it. Their thought processes, their faith. Surely it was more than the mere adoration of kings, though this very region supplied the Khmer, as the ancient Cambodians were called, with an eminent dynasty. Phimai is probably this province's most important edifice from the early

12th century, a time so rich in temple architecture. It is thought to have been constructed before Angkor Wat.

Phimai. The first temple in North East Siam to be restored.

Hinayana Buddhism had been well established by the native Mon peoples since the 7th century, and was adopted by the Thai (meaning southern) peoples of Yunnan who were arriving and settling peacefully in this part of the country from around 1000 AD on. They established small kingdoms which were to become a unified state, superseding the Khmer. In Cambodia the main religion was still Hinduism in the 12th century. Maybe this fusion of Hinduism and Buddhism should be seen in the light of tolerance being an important principle of Buddhism.

Slowly—it was truly hot still, as the late after-noon sun was making the light yellower—we absorbed our first temple after the long drive, wandering about and losing ourselves, almost, behind thick walls. A handful of particularly insensitive tourists also appeared. We let them pass and eventually found our friends again. We sat back on a stone wall and contemplated the grass-covered grounds with the temple in their midst. A large tree gave us shade, and time began to seem immaterial at last.

We had also been to the museum, open to the ele-ments on three sides, where superb lintels are stored and many, many noisy but well-behaved schoolchildren made it *their* building; which indeed it was. They were Thais, after all. They were all beautifully dressed in very dignified blue and white uniforms, loose-fitting mostly, cover-ing gawky limbs, chattering with the enthusiasm of discovery and perhaps just a hint of pride when confronted with a foreigner like me—but no, they were too innocent for that.

We drove on, into what then felt like an illustration of the life they had come from. It was even later in the afternoon now, and children coming back from school mingled with farmers returning home from their fields, walking along the quiet country road at a steady but not hasty pace. They probably had quite long to walk. Flame trees caressed the contours of the almost drably straight lines upon the somewhat monotonous plain, dotted with small villages, everything lovingly kept, in its simple, intelligent way. This is Isaan, supposedly the poorest part of Thailand. Much government investment has flowed into this region to help it, and it has indeed. The last time I was here it was painfully poor, almost unbelievably so, but now everything looks carefully, yet not lavishly, organised. The horrors of the uncontrolled encroachment of the 20th century, as one sees in and around Bangkok and many provincial towns, are absent. Long may it last.

We spent the evening having dinner outside, between a car park and a nightclub. It was the sort of thing one might not have considered as a foreigner. Undoubtedly, as I had noticed before, the willing attention and the excellence of the spicy, tasty Northern food were due to Spha's ordering in Thai.

Breakfast the next day, at the bottom of our extraordinary hotel, the one and only high-rise building in this overgrown country town of Surin, was a buffet: feeding the tired and some-what seedy-looking, mostly young, men, and their companions of the night before; strictly for one night only. This was made quite clear by the fact that the men hardly talked to them, and that the girls submitted demurely to the cold-shoulder treatment. Purely a business transaction, but the girls looked psychologically scarred, bullied into the lowest of expectations. Pale and lifeless under their expertly applied make-up, their eyes were glazed.

Nonetheless, the view from the hotel window when I got up in the morning had been reassuring. A leafy, spread-out city with the typical and rather delightful architecture of official buildings all over Thailand, a link with the Palladio-inspired past in an ever-modernizing country. This used to be the town for rounding up newly found elephants from the surrounding jungle, elephants who were used for work not so long ago—work they performed with great nonchalance. Such was their strength, they carried enormous logs and, in their steady way, with ears flapping like giant fans, they deposited them wherever their mahout, or "elephant driver"—assigned for life, and consequently a great friend—directed them. Their obedience is borne from trust and affection, not fear.

Prasat Phimai after restoration.

Once we left this sprawling country town, with its one tall and ugly building, we really were in the country. The Mun river, moving along like a placid, occasionally wide-girth snake of unknown intentions, could easily be taken for just a collection of shallow lakes, appearing off and on. We are on the ancient road from Phimai to Angkor, with its *barays*, purposefully harnessed reservoirs. In this valley alone there are hundreds of temples, if one can find them. No-one has seen them all. In fact, very few people even knew of their existence until quite recently.

We stopped by a market stall in a tiny town to buy some hats, to the delight and amusement of the locals, who rarely had a chance to see such odd people wanting to buy farmers' hats. When they heard me trying to ascertain a price in Thai, they were even more bewildered. They laughed.

It was hot now, very hot. Standing in the almost mid-day sun was like searing one's brain, it was truly debilitating. But we did now have hats.

And now that we were suitably protected, we arrived at the temple of Sikoraphun, at the end of a long mud path baked by the sun. No-one around. Set in the midst of the flat green country-side were the remainders of what had been a small temple complex, apparently one of importance. It was surrounded by a moat, now empty of water, overgrown by grass. But the spirit of serenity which Buddhist temples emanate was present here too, almost inexplicably so, as there was so little left of the original buildings. The merciless strength of the sun made it hard to focus, but, yes, there were lintels, even *apsaras*—heavenly creatures—perfectly carved yet almost in hiding. And now the slow onset of the spirit of timelessness overcame me, this spirit I had experienced before in Thailand, when in the country, and which always felt like a great blessing. The sacred ruins were partly overlooked by a simple wooden house on the periphery, a check sarong typical of this part of the country hanging up to dry outside. Some cooking pots on a window sill, the house all open. And total silence.

How hot it is. Incredibly hot. It is not the time of year that tourists come to see the ruins. But the people who live here have to, and do, come to terms with the heat. Hence the slow pace, the often spaced-out way of doing things. Doing things fast would be the end of one. And this leads naturally to contemplation, which is not a manifestation of an indulgent or risible lifestyle, as some Europeans assume, but a necessity. The wise way of life of those who have lived here for thousands of years.

It was hard to tear oneself away, but we had much else to see that day and did not know how long the drive would take—especially since driving at night is total madness, with unlit lorries occasionally parked on the road and numerous stories of death by night driving. We had to manage our time responsibly. Long distances, and many temples yet to see.

Kamphaeng Yai, after the sublime abandonment and peace of Sikoraphun, is almost an onslaught.

It stands in the middle of a small, busy town, Baan Kamphaeng Yai, and they are hard to find, both the village and the *prasat*. A prasat is an Indian-inspired temple pyramid, and it forms part of a working temple compound, clad in materials with attention-seeking colours. Alongside the new, the ruined old temple, made of brick, sandstone and laterite, breathes calm and eternity. Grandeur rather than intimacy. The dimensions of its large walls, as its name Yai (great) indicates, are awe-inspiring. In the fierce mid-day sun the exquisitely carved lintels are hard to make out until one has found the right angle to decipher them from. One's eyes are blinded by rays with no consideration even for eyes behind sunglasses. And this is the *cool* season in Thailand's Northeast. It is the end of November now: the very beginning of the cool, dry season.

One grows aware of another reality in this compound, as one flees toward the protection of its immensely old trees, bent slightly, as they are, over the treasure in their midst, protecting us with their cooling shade, away from the glare.

Orange-robed monks walk around purposefully. One of us asks a monk an interested question and he is delighted to explain. He is tall for a Thai, willowy like the trees above us, dignified but not otherworldly. He enjoys talking to a stranger from another continent, another world. Perhaps it breaks up the daily routine, perhaps it is just to have a target for his obvious amiability.

A *wat* is the name for a Thai temple. To see this working *wat*, entwined with the old sanctuary, gives one great hope for the future, for this country whose philosophy of life is Buddhism. The materialism, the opportunism, the grabbing are a reality also; even the exploitation—as in the rest of the world. But perhaps they take another form here.

Gentleness is a highly undervalued quality. It banishes fear. It is consideration, often induced by the practice of meditation. It is a form of grace. On this very site Hinduism was practiced, followed by Buddhism—fervent enough to encourage the construction of a *wat*, a Buddhist temple, for the daily life of a town.

An important statue of a temple guardian was unearthed here during the excavations by the Fine Arts Department; it has been taken away to the National Museum in Bangkok. But a large image of a Buddha seated on a *naga*, the celestial serpent, was also found, and is kept now where it belongs and where it lives on, in the new monastery next to the old walls.

As we cool off under the flame trees and other eminent givers of shade, some little boys come out of the temple school, a small trickle of them, chatting, their faces a mixture of mischievousness, the vulnerability of children and a lust for adventure. They are well cared for, and with what seems to be an underlying awareness. Awareness of the sacred?

The temple sanctuary of Khao Phra Viharn is right on the border of Cambodia. In fact it is considered, controversially, to be inside Cambodia, although the approach to it is found on the Thai side. Crowning a high promontory of the

Dongrek mountains, overlooking an endless expanse of the densely wooded Cambodian plain, much of it disappearing into mist as it sinks into the horizon, the sanctuary is very much in ruins—their fragments speaking of immensely high aesthetic standards. It is an apparition, become stone.

One drives up to it from Sisaket, over several hours, along a newly laid, wide and totally straight road. This takes one across the end of the Khorat plain, the green land and the road virtually entirely empty. It seems to lead nowhere: no signpost to anywhere. As a passenger in the car, I had time to think about reports that the site is still surrounded by minefields, and so very dangerous, having been disputed territory for decades.

It seems strange that Khao Phra Viharn should officially belong to Cambodia, as it is easily, if time-consumingly, reached from the Thai side. It is almost impossible to get to from Cambodia, over whose plains it towers, high upon this spectacular promontory: more than 500 metres high. The ruined, abandoned corpse of an army helicopter on the precipitous slope seems to be there precisely to confirm this, as does the fact that this was the last hiding place of a few Lon Nol troops and their dependents before the country was enslaved by the Khmer Rouge, at the time Phnom Penh had already been overrun. Yet, even though it is no longer theirs, the Thais seem to take good care of it, feeling as they do that the edifice is an expression of their religious and cultural past, as well as that of the Khmer's, and indeed an expression of the present as well. A pragmatic, and a markedly Buddhist, gesture of generosity.

On the way there (we were amongst the first visitors to this previously terror-inducing site) we stopped at a roadside stall, an apparition in this otherwise empty region, with the idea of having some food; a soup was freshly put together for us. Observing the lusty eating, accompanied by flies circulating between ourselves and the open drain, I decided to devote myself to a banana instead. But the drivers and passengers needed feeding, and I was told the soup was excellent.

The makers of the soup and the choppers of vegetables looked at us as extraordinarily exotic foreigners, some of whom spoke Thai nevertheless, travelling with one of their own people who spoke a very distinguished kind of Bangkok Thai, but who also ate the soup (which the roadside cooks had probably eaten for their own meal) with great gusto and appreciation, while not losing too many words about it.

On we drove, black clouds overhanging, partly blocking the illuminating daylight, until finally we were stopped by a forbidding army post, manned by an unexpectedly affable guard to whom we had to hand our passports—not to be returned until *we* did.

A large and empty car park further on; a lot of visitors were obviously expected, but nothing could have breathed more loneliness than this spot. The odd soldier, a Thai and a Cambodian alternatively, appeared and disappeared—certainly not interested in *us*.

Now that we were in Cambodia, the road had ended, and there was barely a path through the only partly-cleared jungle. Then rocks to traverse, covered in graffiti which, illegible for most of us, probably had more to do with war than infatuation. There was a rawness here I was to encounter again on the periphery of Angkor, and even more so inside it. If it had not been so infernally hot it would have sent a shiver down one's spine. We hurried on, not entirely sure where to go, since we had been told they were about to close the gate for the night. The idea of being locked in here energized us enormously. Except for Harvard, who had a sore leg and lagged behind just as we were on the verge of seeing something so fantastic we might not see again for a very long time, if ever. But this was not a peaceful spot. War had done terrible things to it, as one could feel and see. The question as to whether having a Thai speaker leading us was a threat to our security, or a blessing, was resolved when a charming Thai soldier appeared, as we approached the sanctuary. Gently, and at the same time very indulgently, he suggested we hurry.

There is a slow build-up to seeing the temple, as it is approached from ascending staircases with long serpent-guarded causeways in between, each leading to a higher level, a level of which one can see very little from below. The steps are worn and very, very slippery, moss-and lichen-covered like some of the walls. The staircases are wide at first, then narrowing dramatically as they become steeper. The stone is carved rock and had come from nearby quarries, which one can tell from the symmetrical post holes in some of the blocks. The lichen on the stone is a sign not of decay but of pure air, I am told by Harvard, the geologist. These blocks of stone are as deep as they are wide; only an elephant could have carried them, I imagine.

It all starts quite innocently, with vendors under brightly coloured umbrellas lining the first approach. No hard sell here—they are content to chat to each other.

The *nagas*, the symbolic snakes of stone which line the causeways, are immensely long, and are possessors of many heads. They guard the abodes of the gods in a kingdom in which men and animals live side by side, helping each other. Here is also the bull Nadin, transporting the gods Shiva and Uma. And Hanuman, the mischievous and flirtatious monkey god who is ultimately a figure of goodness in the great Hindu epic, the *Ramayana*, which has also been adopted by the Buddhists—a phenomenon to be explored in subsequent pages.

The animals appear and reappear on temple pediments, on balustrades, carved out of stone in temple after temple; and in bas relief, as we were to see later on at Angkor.

Khao Phra Viharn means 'sacred mountain temple' or 'mountain of the sacred temple'. It was enormously hard to tear oneself away from its powerful, graceful presence, the purity of line and dimension in which it culminates. On the way back, elated, one thinks of man's yearning for heaven, for that is where it seemed one had been climbing to—but it was a heaven almost ruined by man, by armed conflict. Yet we wanted to linger, as long as we possibly could. We were made to rush only by the fear of being locked in. A sobering thought. And because the skies were clouding over. Daylight was fading across the Dongrek Range.

Khao Phra Viharn. The sublime purity of line and aura of sanctity that it must have had in the past is still greatly discernible if one manages to visit at a quiet time.

Khao Phra Viharn. The magnificent mountain temple in the process of disintegrating.

The Khmer monuments in Thailand are very weathered and had been neglected for many centuries—until quite recently. They used to be thought of as "provincial Khmer" but new research has brought with it the realisation that this province had been a very important one indeed. The Mun River Valley group of temples is no longer considered a cultural backwater: it may even have been an inspiration for some of the buildings at Angkor. Certainly, of all the Khmer temples I have seen in Thailand, Khao Phra Viharn impressed me the most. There is a greatness of aesthetic standards about it which is overwhelming. It is aloft in its isolation; divine.

The existence of the "Royal Way", an abandoned and almost completely overgrown road which used to link Angkor and Phimai, confirms the significance of this arm of the Khmer empire. It forms a part of a network of roads. From Preah Vihear, as Khao Phra Viharn is called in Cambodia, there runs a straight line east to Champassac, on the Mekhong River in Laos, which must have been another royal road. Very close to this one finds the exquisitely beautiful temple of Wat Phu. Found to have been con-structed as early as the 6th century, it predates the Angkor edifices and the Mun River civilisation in Siam. An inscription from as early as the fifth century AD speaks of King Devanika, a Sanskrit name, and reinforces the evidence of the link with India. Sanskrit, the priestly and scholarly language of Hinduism.

One day, it would be wonderful if peace was a sufficiently permanent feature, if archeologists could get to work on re-establishing this road, linking all the glorious temples and rest houses and hospitals and their chapels on the way. As it was in the 13th century, when pilgrims and travellers used the roads. Khao Phra Viharn itself was first constructed in AD 813, then enlarged and further embellished over the next 300 years.

Wat Phu, which I had seen once on an earlier journey going down the Mekhong River, is incomparable to anything else. Another mountain temple, the gods are approached differently here. Coming from the immense expanse that the Mekhong becomes, thousands of miles from its source in Tibet, its muddy, yellow water almost obliterating the view of the other side, one disembarks at the charming and utterly sleepy country town of Champassac. This, though it certainly does not look it now, is also an ancient settlement. There was even a king of Champassac. Its illustrious past is hard to believe when only a few houses remain, scattered about in a typically haphazard, Asian way. It is functional, yet kept with care and affection, as are the small gardens. At lunch-time, everything is closed; I imagine the inhabitants are hiding from the brutal heat. There is a breeze, though, as I discover when I am taken to a "restaurant" above the bank of the stream. Not far from us, children, without supervision, wade and swim in the cool water, taking pleasure in being silly; their irreverence is refreshing. But the older ones do also take responsibility for their smaller brothers and sisters, often carrying them. No acts of bravado, though. Like children brought up in the mountains, they respect the superior strength of the elements, and stay close to the shore.

Coming from Pakse, a market town further up the river, a highway takes one down to a landing stage, where one is sent across by ferry. This one consists of a few wooden planks tied together on top of three former Russian gunboats which, I am glad to see, have found a rather more useful second existence. There is space for two cars and a few passengers. It is a delightfully timeless experience, drifting across, our direction corrected here and there by the thrust of the engine.

One continues by road, alongside the mighty, slow-moving Mekhong. And then one finds oneself in front of a languidly rising mountain, with ruined *viharas*—monastic buildings—on either side, looking identifiably Khmer. A generously proportioned reservoir, or *baray*, always part of a Khmer temple, indicates the relative importance of the site. Tall trees mirror themselves in the still water. The baray is virtually full even though we are nearing the end of the dry season, before the ample monsoon rainfall replenishes this and the many others which will have dried out. Maybe they were used for rice irrigation in times of need; maybe they were purely symbolic.

But it is the slow climb to the mountaintop which is the culmination of the experience. Either side of the wide staircase, a sea of frangipani trees lines the way, with more ruins to explore alongside, all covered in white lichen. The tree trunks are covered in lichen, too, giving them a sense of timelessness. And then at the top, where the sacred Hindu symbols of the *linga* and the *yoni* are to be seen, one finally turns round. Below is the truly heavenly site of Wat Phu, lined by the white blossoms of the frangipani, the water basins further below, the immense plain and finally the huge river beyond, all laid out before one. A more wonderful position for a temple would be hard to find. It takes one's breath away. One longs to stay. It appears to one as a link between nature and the divine.

Wat Phu, the frangipani-framed staircase leading up to
the source of holy water.

A spring donates ample water to those wishing to
have their soul purified. We let it run over our
faces, if only to cool down in the heat of the afternoon. The ritual gives a feeling of elation, even to
me, who does not know of most of the religious
connotations. This temple complex was built by
Hindus; now Buddhists worship here. But the

symbolism of the purity and the life-giving quali-
ties of a mountain spring are obvious. The last
kings of Laos used to come here on a pilgrimage
and attend the Festival held during the February
full moon, together with many other Laotian
Buddhists. I would love to do so, too, one day,
before it is too late and it becomes a tourist site.

Approach to the inner sanctum of the temple complex.

Lintel depicting Indra, god of the sky and of rain, carried
by the three-headed elephant Erawan.

Fully-armed temple guardian.

Upriver lies the old capital of Laos, Luang Prabang: a conglomeration of superlatively beautiful Buddhist temples and innumerable stupas (or chedis, as they are called here), in an unhurried town overlooking the Mekhong. The King used to live here. Towards the end of the Vietnam War he was sent into the jungle by the Pathet Lao with his wife and sons, to be re-educated as a communist. Because he was old and he could not work, his rations were halved. His eldest son offered him half of his rice, but he refused it. So his son, who was also his heir, made him eat. But in the end the son himself died, before his father, and his mother. It sounds like a fairy tale by Oscar Wilde, but it is no fairy tale.

There are more temples than anything else in Luang Prabang, it had seemed to me, when I first went there just before the Communist takeover in 1974. But those temples deserve another book. Being there was to me an aesthetic and spiritual revelation. Nonetheless, the fragility of the mood could already be felt by then. Alongside the happily playing children were young soldiers—extremely young, not older than fourteen, perhaps sixteen. They looked ready to use the heavy guns they carried so defiantly. All this is a long time ago now, but the effects have not altogether vanished.

And downriver, where the Mekhong fans out beyond the horizon, lie the Three Thousand Islands. Dreamy islands. They lie in the now immensely wide river, carrying what seems like half the mud of the globe's surface in its waters. And then comes the Cambodian border.

Back in Thailand, we were to spend the night in Sisaket, where a rural kind of 20th century awaited us. A slow-moving country town of mostly recent construction with, I think, one hotel, we appeared to be the only guests. Or so it seemed. Our travelling companions Spha and

Manuela had a rare and highly romantic anniversary to celebrate: thirty years of mutual devotion and, indeed, matrimony. The champagne equivalent from a family vineyard in Italy had been laboriously kept cold in the Jeep, all the way; waiting for this. Having been told that there was no dining-room in the hotel, we "celebrated" in the nightclub, where the most astounding number of singers entertained remarkably few guests. The effect was alienating. One wondered why there were so many to choose from. To crown this amazing performance, the Thai food we had ordered turned out to be so fiercely hot that the taste of the celebratory wine mostly evaporated under the onslaught. Talking was almost impossible because of the deafening music. All we could do was laugh at our mutual incomprehension and at the extraordinary setting for the great event. And then there were the chillies. The conspiracy was complete.

The temple sanctuaries of Prasat Phnom Rung and Muang Tam, which we were to visit next, lie on another axis of the pilgrimage road—but they are a long way away from the celestial sweep of gables at Khao Phra Viharn. They are of more human dimensions, as if forgiving of human frailty. One can love them more easily.

When we did reach Phnom Rung the following day, we were halfway between Phimai and

Angkor along the Royal Road, although we had of course travelled on a perfectly modern country highway. Prasat Phnom Rung is another mountain-top temple of great nobility, with a rich and inspiring history. The local dynasty supplied several of Angkor's kings and were much more than mere vassals. They probably supported them in military campaigns. Illustrating this, a battle fought on elephant back can be seen carved out on a pediment. Having successfully supported his great king (and relative) in battle, Narendraditya, the local ruler under whom Phnom Rung was built, renounced war and became a monk, and a guru. King Suryavarman II, whom he had helped in battle, went on to build Angkor Wat.

Prasat Phnom Rung has been restored for 17 years. The result is a temple which looks as it would have done when newly constructed, or very nearly. Even the tall, upright stone figure of a temple guardian stands in its original place, a rare sight indeed by now, when most statues have vanished from their originally intended places. This restoration is the most art-historically correct in the Mun river valley, I was told by a guide years later. It is also considered the most important and inspiring temple complex in this region.

As we arrived at midday, we first fortified ourselves with some very good Som Tam, the green papaya salad so perfectly and refreshingly prepared in the Northeast. By the extensive parking lot leading up to the site there are quite a few places to eat, places to sit in the shade for a while, something one needs to do to clear the mind, to be receptive for what is to come.

Prasat Phnom Rung was a Hindu temple and is now venerated by Buddhists. One encounters small, dispersed groups of Thai visitors here and there, walking at the slow pace dictated by the heat, a phenomenon that perhaps helps meditation, too. Walking at the right pace, one is slowly overcome by a sense of peace, which increases when one rests altogether. There must be no noise. Buddhism without tranquility is unthinkable.

Again steps lead up to the sanctuary, preceded by an exquisite sandstone naga bridge; these five-headed nagas have been in situ since the 12th century, symbolizing a bridge between the world we live in and the divine.

The intricately carved lintels and pediments tell imaginary Hindu tales of the lives of the divinities. There is a missing lintel here and there, indicative of many more gaps to come at other sites. Manuela tells me of the launching of negotiations by Silpakorn University's Professor Prince

Subhadradis Diskul, negotiations to ensure the return of the lintel of the reclining Vishnu, called the Phra Narai Lintel, which is meant to be above the mandapa entrance. The lintel had mysteriously disappeared as the temple was nearing restoration. His negotiating skills achieved the return of this important support across a door: important for the unity of the buildings and the cultural cohesion of its place of birth. So, as it turns out, the Art Institute of Chicago was not quite the place it was meant to remain, however open-minded one might be …

Above an entrance, the evocative scene of battle by elephant brings to life the importance of these beasts in Khmer life a thousand years ago. No wonder they were revered as sacred beasts, particularly the albinos, more courteously called 'white elephants'. They were considered the automatic property of the king, and were held in even greater esteem than "ordinary" elephants. Even now one can see them at work in this part of the world, carrying logs; they are much more than merely decorative.

To sit and chat with really good friends on the hill of Prasat Phnom Rung, saying less and less, and eventually letting silence overtake one, brought about a sense of fulfillment. One felt at peace with the world, and very close to one's companions, finally without a word being spoken.

Temple guardian with donated flower.

Five-headed naga, one of many, guarding
PHNOM RUNG.

From Prasat Phnom Rung down to Muang Tam is only a short drive on what used to be one of the most important royal roads to Angkor. The architectural layout of Muang Tam resembles the design of a quincuncial jewel, perfect in its symmetry.

At first approach one walks under tall trees and sees their crowns reflected in symmetric ponds of water, dark and serene. The still water is almost entirely covered by green leaves crowned with fluorescent pink lotus flowers: very healthy specimens. They strike one as expressions of a joie de vivre not unlike that emanating from a floating angel on the wall of a High Baroque church. I was reminded of the sight at Lopburi, an old capital of Siam further south, and a rarely visited one: the sight of seemingly endless pools of water nourishing these holy flowers, so meaningful in

Buddhism, as they stretched through rice fields towards a high horizon. Seeing the great profusion of these lotuses brings one to the realization of where the strong, vibrant colours of the local textiles come from, so unexpected to someone brought up to European taste, as restrained and muted as it is by comparison.

It has been written that the four ponds represent the four oceans surrounding Mount Meru, the center of the universe in Hindu mythology and in Buddhist belief: it is where the Gods live. After this wonderfully sensitive restoration was completed, I heard, a concert had been given here— what a heavenly place for music. How I wished I had been there.

But to sit at an entrance, or upon a low, naga-crested wall, watching the lotuses slowly close their petals for the night, brings one closer to eternity, and creation. The moat is a symbol of the ocean that surrounds us. Both Gnung Agung, the volcano that towers over Bali, and the Himalayas are representative of Mount Meru, lying in the sea of water, the Ocean of Infinity. The serpent-cloud surrounding the Mountain is represented by the nagas. Contemplating this spectacle of nature, I promise myself next time to come back in the morning, so I can see the flowers unfold. Laughter and joyful children's noises, coming from the village school close to the temple, bring one back to life, to now. As we leave the enclosure, the pupils stand in the schoolyard for assembly, and then they sing. All out in the open, under a benevolent blue sky.

Muang Tam from the interior.

A five-headed naga guards the confines of the basins of precious life-giving water, not only decorative and symbolic, but also the basis of Khmer agricultural wealth.

The water basins, covered in water lilies.

But half an hour later, as we drove down the hillside that gave its name to Phnom Rung, the firmly-closed windows of the Jeep were lashed furiously by rain from a cloudburst that lasted hours. A narrow, winding road snaked downhill through more rain, and then, quite suddenly, an apparition of the brightest possible sunlight manifested itself—a wonder, and a transformation that occurs only in the tropics. Within the clear light, persecution from feelings of foreboding evaporates, and hope is possible again. As we drive on, now on a wider, straighter, more important road meant to lead us to Khorat, black clouds gather again. Another downpour chases us while it slowly begins to get dark. The end of the day. Small dogs emerge from the side of the road from time to time, waiting, or walking somewhere at the slow pace the moist heat commands. Sitting in this rain—drenched cage of a car, advancing with headlights along a lonely country road, I now know exactly where I want to be and who I want to be with for the rest of my life, if it is to be a life worth living. An intense yearning overcomes me and recedes again as the rain finally turns to dribble and then backs off, making room for a clear night as we reach the confines of the now-large city of Khorat. Nakhon Ratchasima, as it is also called, was a sleepy country town not so

long ago, but it has become the booming metrop-
olis of the Northeast and appears coldly ruthless
in comparison to the still dormant territory of
rural Isaan, which we had only just left. We ate
expertly prepared Chinese food in a practically
deserted high-rise hotel with cosmopolitan pre-
tensions. And we slept in comfortable beds.

Back in Bangkok, the old cynicism kicks in again
and—wow—the patience one needs, wading
through the late rush-hour traffic on a Friday
afternoon before a long weekend. And, studying
the faces behind the wheels, people *are* patient,
much more than they would be in a similar situa-
tion in Europe. And then, the soothing pleasure
of being welcomed into a well-run family home

once again, run by people one knows, and who remember one, after the anonymity of different hotels every night.

Drinks: in the sala, a raised open platform with an ornamental (and protective) Thai roof which overlooks the garden. It is getting dark. A few dogs bark, and a long way away the din of city life subsides, slowly, to a more easy-going level. And a swim: the great luxury of a tropical country, at the end of a long and exhausting day.

The next day tables are being laid ceremoniously inside for a party. The Thai women look splendid in their antique weaves and embroideries, their fine jewels; they show their admirable composure.

I sit between Spha, by now recovered from the long days of driving, and Mark—old friends all three of us. Much laughter results, references which are hard to follow by others. And a new awareness of the precious nature of friendship emerges as if by magic. Mark chooses his words carefully, he who had used them as hammer blows in the past.

Long after the other guests have gone, we continue to sit and chat. Mark is unable to tear himself away for a long time, there is too much for him to say. And I am touched and delighted by the re-emergence of this rapport of many years past.

It is indeed hard to leave early the day after to get onto the plane to Siem Reap, in Cambodia, in order to visit Angkor. But we get there, quite uneventfully. The Grand Hotel is exquisite—an invitation to drinks from the manager arrives in a wooden box filled with chocolates, embossed with a silver portrait of an elephant. The trampled ancient graciousness and the culture are still alive, are being further resurrected. The old Asia is still alive, if only just. There are glimpses of it everywhere: the more unintentional they are, the more evocative.

"Everyone here has lost someone" says Gilbert Madhavan, the manager, referring to his staff and to their families' sufferings under the Khmer Rouge, when I point out how thoughtful, how gentle they are. He does not go into details, nor is this the time to do so. He gives us champagne, which must be a great extravagance in Siem Reap, where everything that people from the West require must be flown in. Maybe when Cambodia was still a French colony this was standard practice, at least at special moments. Either way, it is good to have, as is the late night reading selection, about the days of Angkor's first restorations, left on one's pillow, adding another dimension to what one had seen during the day. Or sharpening one's imagination for the next.

The men and women who serve in the restaurant had no aura of compliant sexual knowledge about them, as is sometimes seen in Asia. They were very thin, to the point of being ethereally beautiful at times, and they possessed a dignity of a kind only great catharses can induce. Yet they did not suggest any sadness. Maybe they were no longer Buddhist, having been forcefully re-educated, but centuries of a Buddhist way of life and its beliefs had given them strength of a kind one rarely observes.

Walking through the bar to meet Mr. Madhavan, I come to a corner hall between the annexe and the original building, modern and open to the elements at the sides, perfectly combining the neo-colonial architecture of the original structure from 1929 with the newly built additions. All sorts of preparations are under way in the small pavilion, including the floating of blossoms in the water "bassins", a ritual reminiscent of Loy Krathong, the Buddhist festival of light. It is partly for the opening of an exhibition of photographs by Jaroslav Poncar, who works at Angkor on a programme of the University of Applied Sciences of Cologne, restoring the apsaras, celestial female beings and dancers carved of stone, which form an important part of temple architecture. It is a visual delight. Not knowing who he is,

Harvard starts a conversation with him, and we are invited to visit the site and office of the German Apsara Conservation Project the next morning.

The cage-like site is so well locked up we almost despair of finding our way in, but eventually we do, tentatively let in by a sullen-faced guard. Professor Hans Leisen, the project director, is expecting us; he gives us a good welcome and shows us round. He is in fact very unprofessorial, and it turns out that we have a friend in common who makes films in Munich and whose visit he is expecting soon. The set-up is simple and seemingly unstructured (due to lack of money, the usual problem). One must admire them for working under such conditions. Yet they are driven by their own great enthusiasm and their devotion to the cause. They pass their expertise on to their Cambodian assistants, so that one day they can take over. From outside we look into a large shed, fully fenced in, which is filled with apsaras, the heavenly creatures in stone which were stolen and have been brought back here to be restored. They are brought in sometimes from the back of lorries speeding towards the border. They are able only to capture and house a minimal number of the statues in danger of leaving the country, their means being so limited. It may be an endless task. The antique shops in Bangkok, Paris and New York are well stocked, and a great deal of private dealing in these looted objects goes on. One hears so many stories it is hard to know what to believe, but after speaking with Hans Leisen I realize that even the most horrifying must be true.

It was Mr. Heng who collected us at the airport, and who became our guide. He had been a monk, but the Khmer Rouge had chased him away from that (to them) useless existence; they chased him into the fields, without telling him what to do and how he should do it. No tools, of course. His features, his skin and his badly damaged teeth reflect the disdain for humanity by those obsessed with the grabbing and retaining of power, whose ruthlessness was considered an honorable quality (in their eyes). But he only rarely and reluctantly speaks of it.

When, on the first morning out with him, he begins to instruct us, he starts with the usual litany of facts and national "achievements" that is thrown at one in totalitarian countries—travels in Burma and Russia come to mind. But once he has done his "duty" as required, he realizes, at first tentatively, that we prefer a more contemplative pace to the machine-gun delivery of speech; he is now prepared to put the occasional pause into his eloquence. In fact, he was such a good guide that the three days we had meant to stay became a week, and still we felt that there was so much more to see.

At the time of seeing Angkor one holds one's breath impatiently for more and more.
In retrospect, one is simply overwhelmed.

As one approaches the Angkor Wat complex, one emerges from virtually straight roads lined by high old trees, planted not at random, but symmetrically. The interlinking roads are incredibly reminiscent of treelined *allées* and country roads in France, and at the same time of the precise layout of formal French gardens. This net of gentle symmetry is crowned by the first view of the temple of Angkor Wat, towering above the vast moat, which at the time of its greatest splendour must have been alive with water lilies or lotus flowers. The roads, constructed by French colonials (or was it the archeologists?) fit like a suitable frame around the great temple, distant and unapproachable as it at first appears. A long, long naga-bridge leads up to it, and one longs and somehow fears to go all the way up to it; we do not have the time. Instead, a site of pathetic horror. A man on a motorcycle swiftly driving past us is carrying, on his luggage rack, an enormous live pig, far too large for the bike. The pig is fastened to the rack lying on its side, a spine-breaking proposition, especially at this speed and over the potholes. It screams in horror, the most terrifying screams. The man drives on. Obviously the pig had the wrong social origins.

It takes a while to recover from this and to concentrate on aesthetics again, but, the human mind being flexible, one can. We stop in front of a large ruin which from afar had looked like photographs of Dresden after the war—but from close up is revealed to be a monument to the genius and the inspired eye of the Khmer who built it. This is The Bayon. It, and we, are drenched in blinding sunlight, so much so it is difficult to see where one is going. There is so much of it. The layout becomes a mystery once one is inside. I admire Mr. Heng for taking us to see first of all something that is quite simply wonderful. The bas-reliefs at the Bayon, which must be the second most important, if not the most important temple in this ancient capital, surpass those at Angkor Wat in their poetic expression and vivacity. They move one, depicting the people and their lives with the animals, as well as the gods and kings and armies of Angkor. Without a powerful and wise king, the life of the people would have been fraught with danger, restless and unhappy.

Even though these were the first bas-reliefs we saw, and we could not yet compare them to those of Angkor Wat itself, one simply felt in the presence of genius, of an overwhelmingly humane interpretation of life.

Those were the praised bas reliefs, far too many of them to take in on a first visit. Spurred on by curiosity, we eventually followed Mr Heng into the inner part, expectantly and unquestioningly, like dogs their master. *There* were the giant heads of the supposed god-kings. At first sight I found them repellent. They are gigantic within the scale of the edifice and, sinister looking, they dominate it from above. No fine features on their immense heads, just better-knowing, cynical smiles. Expressions of ruthlessness. They made me want to turn away—but perhaps they were meant to appear as protectors, in the sense of the fanged monsters that are the temple guardians? The crude imagery of this in the film *Apocalypse Now*, a director's ego trip, had years ago evoked disdain and horror in me towards these heads, so maybe I was prejudiced. Perhaps there is an explanation to this misunderstanding of iconography, but so far I am ignorant of it.

On our way back to Siem Riep we pass picnickers and food stalls on the open ground facing Angkor Wat. They are lunching at a respectful distance. No clutter, Asian style, anywhere near the monument. There has to be a niche for real life somewhere here if the local people, or Cambodians from far and wide, are to come and admire what has been theirs for over a thousand years. Asians, with their love of eating at all times, of making themselves part of what goes on around them.

There is something soothing about the fact that this everyday activity should take place not that far from such immense grandeur.

All over Asia, not far from, or sometimes in the midst of the perfect symmetry of architecture, one finds this village mentality: people chatting, eating, buying, being friendly and outgoing; not only because it is part of their self-appointed job to sell, but also as an expression of their natural exuberance, and often of female independence too. The big businessmen in Thailand are frequently women; their husbands tend to be administrators. And Chinese women, of course, are legendary for their enterprising nature.

When Jon Swain described Phnom Penh, the capital of Cambodia, as it was before the horrors of the Vietnam War descended upon it, it sounded quintessentially South-East Asian in its languorous existence, infused with the humane-ness of Buddhism and, at the same time, its bub-bly enthusiasm and eagerness. The playfulness of South-East Asia: a balm for heavily laden European hearts, weighed down by grey weather and a culture of accusations.

Mr Heng, having got the official messages of duty out of his system, now wordlessly leads us from temple to temple. He leaves us to contemplate, while he is always nearby and ready with an explanation if wanted. When we admire the rows and rows of sublimely beautiful, deliciously breasted apsaras in the Terrace of the Leper King, Mr Heng sighs deeply. He says he would like to have a wife. I wonder if he really means a wife, or a lover—a notion forbidden in Communist thinking. But then wives can be lovers too. The hypocritical prudery of Communist dogma brings back the old cynicism, even in so sublime a place.

The temple complex of Bantey Srei is so often considered to be the culmination of what is beautiful in Angkor-related architecture. When we finally get there, after the driver had paid off some nasty-looking hang-abouts—armed, I'm sure—we find the small temple of Bantey Srei. It is positively crawling with, mostly, Japanese tourists, who look at nothing but photograph everything—as tourists tend to do. No statues left any more here. Filigree lintels, everything in miniature, or so it seems. This temple predates Angkor Wat by 200 years. The sculptural refinement is affecting but, sadly, the onslaught of human bodies and their cameras devastates all that is inspiring about it. At least on this day.

But anger is ugly: it is part of the passion Buddhist teaching urges us to live without. For good reason. So far the world has survived, despite an apparently unstoppable chain of acts of retribution. But for how much longer? Without a will for forgiveness—Christian thinking says so too—we will have to live in fear, always. Fear of annihilation by *some*one, as we are all guilty of *some*thing, whatever it may be.

I have a theory about Bantey Srei's origins. It might have been constructed as a reminder by one or several architects who had been totally struck by elation at seeing Preah Vihear. It could not have been the same architect, as one who had been capable of such greatness of construction would refuse to see it erected in a diminutive form. To me, Preah Vihear is the more beautiful temple. Its proportions are awe-inspiring. Bantey Srei, which is vaguely contemporary with it, seems relatively sugary by comparison. Of course, Preah Vihear is not part of the Angkor complex. But it was part of the kingdom.

I am just as much at a loss for words as Somerset Maugham was in the late 1920s, when he wrote *The Gentleman in the Parlour* and reached Angkor after a tortuous journey, mostly by boat. He had only recently recovered from malaria, and it had nearly finished him off. I was spared these hardships, and I did not arrive in front of the Wat in the middle of the night, as he did, but in the calm daylight of a December morning. Yet the effect was just as overpowering.

To compose a symphony of words to accompany such an architectural apparition, to reproduce it on a page, is quite beyond my capacity, and it is wonderful to read how even Maugham gave up on the impossible task. Just to think of doing it …

Having crossed the long causeway over the abundant moat, meant to resemble the cosmic ocean, we reach the sacred monument, dedicated to Vishnu. We are immediately taken to see the famed bas-reliefs, the longest in the world. Carved finely into the walls are scenes from the *Ramayana* and highly ritualistic battle scenes from the *Mahabharata*, the other great Indian epic. Here is the image of "The Churning of the

Ocean of Milk", representing eternal life; and the creation of the universe. Oh so many apsaras, all lovely, but some of them greatly abused by the Khmer Rouge soldiers who had made the temple their hide-out every now and then. Apsaras are celestial beings who love water—nymphs. Hence Angkor Wat, with its extensive moat, is just the place for them. The thought of how much the soldiers despised and abused them, though, is chilling to behold.

Luckily there is much, much more to be absorbed by, as we wander past images of various Hindu deities, and sculptural friezes depicting the life of the then king; and followed by Yama, god of death …

For the first time in my life I am suddenly struck by vertigo, as I stand at the top of yet another extremely steep and slippery staircase, looking down on the immense plain strewn with the remains of temples, and onto the absorbing jungle. For about ten minutes I cannot climb down, I am riveted to the stairs, I cannot speak. I blame the malaria drug for it, which I also found can exaggerate sounds. But then I see a young Cambodian mother with a small child experiencing the same phenomenon, staggering while the child is unaffected. All the others simply climb down. It has never happened to me again.

Magnificent though it is, there is something frightening about Angkor Wat, eerily and not entirely logically highlighted by recent Cambodian history. There is a theory that Angkor Wat might have been built as a funerary temple, and it does seem plausible. Time is transmuted when one stands at the top of Angkor Wat, the jungle looking on, waiting, from beyond the moat.

The temple monastery of Ta Prohm has been left in the state it was found, having been spared restoration. One can only just guess the outlines of the vast monastic complex. Trees overgrow it, overhang it, pushing the heavy walls apart with their superior force. A powerful reminder that nature is stronger than man's work, without trying. The sculpture-encrusted walls from the Classic period of the 12th century intermingling with the giant tree roots growing out of them give an unearthly, fairy-tale quality to the complex. As one knows, there are not only enchanted but also evil creatures in fairy-tales. I am vividly reminded of this by a shadowy-looking man with an axe who appears quite suddenly out of the depths of the temple, blindingly overgrown with vegetation as it is. He wears the chequered scarf of the Khmer Rouge around his neck and shoulders. He is large, and he scowls at us. Does he have a gun, too, or does he prefer axes? He shoos us away with what seems a threatening gesture. Maybe he is just warning us of landmines; perhaps we are disturbing him in his work of clearing the jungle? A hopeless task, I would imagine. He could almost be a phantom—but he looks too real, and he mutters something we cannot understand.

Nonetheless, we continue to immerse ourselves in this maze of stone and vegetation as if we are hypnotized. For a purist, this is utter perfection. The arrogance of man in what he considers his creation is given a severe blow here. But quite apart from that, the visual impact of Ta Prohm evokes powerful emotions. One lets go of all that one has learnt in the process of visiting the temples; it no longer matters. One is overwhelmed by a completely different kind of beauty. The jungle no longer stands back, keeping watch, as it did around the restored temples. Here we are surrounded by the jungle, lost to it, dazed by it.

It makes one realize also what Angkor would have looked like to the French explorers and archeologists when they first arrived, and what genii they were. And, finally, what human imagination, backed by the powerful finances of a wealthy nation, is able to achieve. How comforting that there are things for countries to spend money on other than war.

Ta Prohm is so beautiful, one has problems tearing oneself away. Even while walking away from it, one longs to return. And we did return another day, to find it much less threatening and even more beautiful.

"There are undiscovered temples, still to be found," says Mr Heng. When I remark on the absence of birds, he says that they were eaten, and that "the wild animals ran away in the fighting". Aside from the destruction caused by war one becomes fearful of haphazard overdevelopment, which could be just as destructive. One temple we visited was overrun, visibly destroyed by visitors and disdainful neglect. The barays, those large water reservoirs the Khmer built everywhere, which fed a net of canals for agricultural irrigation, look mostly dry. The rainy season had ended not *that* long ago.

As if to make up for this disenchantment, Mr Heng takes us to an active Buddhist temple in the grounds of Angkor Wat. Since the ousting of the Khmer Rouge, Buddhism is once again the state religion in Cambodia. They tried to abolish it, and the monks were killed in the process. But I am grateful that Mr Heng has been spared, only just spared though he was. The recently-built temple that we visit is poor and simple by comparison to, say, a temple in Thailand, but is all the more touching for it. The monks are men possibly at their most mischievous age, yet they are docile, inward-looking, appearing idealistic and fearless, as opposed to the soldiers, the tools of destruction, they might have become. Seeing them stride out so purposefully, their taut, elastic bodies infused with dignity, revives one's belief in humanity. By taking us here after we had seen all the glorious temples of the past, Mr Heng has shown us that he realizes we care. We are thankful.

When I walk past the hotel bookshop, I spot The Cambodia Daily and pick it up to read while having breakfast on the terrace. There, on the front page of the somewhat thin newspaper, is a photograph of Preah Vihear. Peace negotiations have been held there, I read. And the result is the final defection of the Khmer Rouge commanders and their remaining troops. The word "defanged" is aptly used about them. It is Monday, December 7, 1998. A new era is to begin. And I am overcome with the realization of how completely unaware I was of the outside world whilst here at Angkor.

I needed something to remind me of Angkor, something of value. When I ask Mr Heng to take me to buy some of the beautiful silk I had seen in the hotel, he takes me, after much prodding, to the market. Not the tourist market, as he points out, but the market where the inhabitants of Siem Riep buy their fruit and vegetables. There are only two stands for textiles, one of a much higher standard than the other. Superb weaves in the traditional Court patterns, the silk of good, thick quality, in exquisitely subtle colour combinations, surpassing those at the hotel by a long way. They are from Phnom Penh, the capital, the vendor says. She is almost reluctant to sell. Maybe she wonders if a mere foreigner is deserving enough to own such works of art. No doubt the patterns have a special significance within the framework of the old Cambodian lifestyle. I still have the silk I bought then, and every now and then I take it out and look at it. I was reluctant to have anything made from it, in case something went wrong and the material were spoilt. I know no dressmaker who would be aware of what a treasure these silks were.

As we leave, we walk past a horrifying number of cripples, begging. Landmine victims, probably. They look quite incredibly poor. A truly impoverished society that cannot look after the suffering. There are many landmines left still. Cambodia has the largest number of prosthesis-requiring people in the world. A present from visiting nations.

Long before the French explorers arrived in Cochin China there were Chinese and Japanese pilgrims to Angkor. The Chinese diplomat Zhou Daguan, who arrived at Angkor in 1296, even left an exhaustive, chatty chronicle on the subject. His *Memoirs of the Customs of Cambodia* is to this day the prime source of information on life in the kingdom's Classic age. There were merchant-pilgrims then, too. And now there are people like me, people who seek to know. Are we just pious tourists, or are we pilgrims, too? If it is supposed to be an act of Buddhist devotion to go and visit temples, which it is, then perhaps we are. One feels a never-ending, ever-increasing desire to find and to see more and more of these divine places. Sometimes it is only in finding things that one knows one has been looking for them.

It may be confusing to have Hindu gods like Vishnu and Shiva inhabit Buddhist temples, but Buddhism came from Brahmanic Hinduism, and temples dedicated to Hindu gods were later to become Buddhist. While Hindus believe in asceticism as an ideal, Buddhists aspire to the "Middle Way". Obviously there is a lot more to either belief, which can be found in the relevant books. In many temples in Theravada Buddhist South East Asia both faiths exist side by side, exhibiting tolerance. They build on each other, as they did at Angkor, where Hindu and Buddhist works are at times hard to distinguish from one another. Both religions were practiced simultaneously. Theravada (or Singhalese) Buddhism is a congregational religion, and the Sangha, the community of monks (and just a few nuns) are highly respected by all. It was, and in some countries still is, they who educate children and perform rituals, much as it was in Christian countries in the past,

and still can be. They are in many ways the back-
bone of the country, giving it stability and the
mysticism the human soul requires.

So I continued my search for enlightenment over
many years, in many countries in Asia. But I was
longing to return to Sukothai, which had
enchanted me in 1973 and which I heard had now
been reconstructed as a Historical Park. Unlike in
1973, when I travelled by road, I took a plane to
Sukothai's new airport. We landed right next to a
pond full of waterlilies, brilliantly pink and looking very healthy, as they do only in Thailand. One
proceeds to a building I had presumed to be a

hotel or private residence, but no: it is the open-air arrival hall, spacious and uncluttered, yet intimate enough for a small airport. Kind hands load one's cases onto chariots and are gone again before one can tip. By contrast, some of the small airports in the Caribbean come to mind, where one is treated like cattle, snarled at and made to queue forever, so as better to appreciate the stagnant heat that the inappropriate cement buildings hold. And where one has to cajole people into doing their job.

The hotel is a great counterpoint. Vast, forbiddingly empty, like a state-run hotel in a totalitarian country. Even the food is barely edible, and that is saying something in this country of culinary delights. Well, I had not come here for the hotel.

We take bicycles to tour the ancient city of Sukothai, which once was the capital of the kingdom of the same name. The art of Sukothai is often considered to be the very height of Siamese art. It is Thai in character, as opposed to Khmer, Burmese, Lanna (from the Northern kingdom), or that of the Andaman isthmus running down to Malaysia in the South.

Wat Mahathat. At first approach, stupas, crumbling walls and reliquary shrines, known as *chedis*. Quite a few Buddhas look upon us. One draws near it by crossing what must once have been a moat, now a grassy subsidence, past the temple grounds' surrounding wall and onto further grassy surfaces. At one point the grounds contained hundreds of religious buildings. Years ago we picnicked by an abandoned lotus pond by the great Buddha we are now drawn to again, as if by magnet. We approach it haltingly, not wanting to dissipate the moment of premonition. I had seen it before restoration, and never forgotten it.

Waterlilies abound; within the restored pond a very small temple sits upon a grassy mound. It seems that one walks too fast. One slows down. As is appropriate, the essence of Buddhism being contemplation.

The Buddha blesses, one and all. The divine presence is all-pervading, as it is in the great Buddhist monuments of Burma's Pagan, Borobodur in Java, Pollonaruwa in Sri Lanka. And even Taxila in northern Pakistan, although there is nothing left there of the Ghandaran art it inspired (except for a rather pathetic museum). Nonetheless, the setting has, miraculously, retained a deeply peaceful aura. Even along the Karakoram Highway, towards the Himalayas, there are remains of the stelae and occasional rock carvings left behind by Buddhists.

The Thais only arrived at what was then called Sukhodaya in the 13th century. The original inhabitants of these fertile river plains, perfect for planting rice, were the Mon, who intermarried with peaceful arrivals from Yunnan in southern, that is Tai, China. The Mon were Hinayana Buddhists and, having superseded the ruling Khmer, the Thais slowly adopted their religion and created small kingdoms in the area, such as Sukhothai. Theravada Buddhism then arrived from Sri Lanka and took over. The Mon base, as well as the Khmer and Burmese influences, created the uniquely Thai art forms we can still admire here today. The Burmese were the conquerors by the 16th century, starting in the north.

Not far away is Si Satchanalai, connected to Sukothai by another royal road, the Phra Ruang. Si Satchanalai was the seat of the deputy king of Sukothai and was at times equally as important. What remains of it is miraculously unchanged.

As we drive up to the first temple, Wat Chang Lom, we are greeted, auspiciously, by a waiting elephant. We feed him sugarcane and bananas, as suggested by his mahout, and we let the wonderful absence of people in this heavenly place engulf us. Tall, centuries-old trees shield us from too much sun. The first stupa we are taken to is surrounded by a garland of elephants in stone, though most have had their tusks inexplicably destroyed by the invading army from Burma. Envy, perhaps. After visiting many ancient monuments one inevitably comes to the conclusion that it does not really matter who did which evil deed, who sought to damage whom. Senseless destruction is always the same, anywhere in the world.

The stone elephants look straight at one in the mellow afternoon light, in a strange, benign sort of way. They must have seen so much—quite apart from witnessing their own wild herds dwindling increasingly, though wild elephants are still reputed to be in the area. Elephants are the sacred beasts of the Hindu and especially of the Buddhist kingdoms. It is easy to see why they are held in such esteem when one watches them quite casually munching whole trees, all the while keeping up their firm, adaptive gait; their philosophical air.

The so-called 'Historical Park of Si Sathanalai' is as enchanting to visit as Sukothai was when I first penetrated it, long before its restoration was begun. There have been no efforts at "improvement", and all the better for it. There are only mud paths to lead one; having left one's vehicle, one wanders easily from one shrine to the next, at a suitably meditative pace. One's tempo is dictated in part by the immense heat and the calming influence of the towering trees, as, too, by a kind of moss covering the ground, cushioning one's steps; and by the absence of creatures—until I catch sight of a kingfisher landing on the branch of a tree, the greenish blue of its wings turning to royal blue: a glorious colour. This bird must be one of the great wonders of nature. Seeing it in this serene, natural setting—man's creation subdued by nature, true, yet nonetheless in harmony with it—recalls one's sense of wonder at the creation of life. Kingfishers are rare now; they probably always were rare, as the Chinese went so far as to make filigree-mounted hair ornaments and other jewels out of the great delicacy of their feathers. One hopes they were not killed in the process, but we will leave that to the Chinese. Kingfisher blue comes up often on cloisonné works of art, too: they show a great preference for the colour. It has taken me a long time to realize where the inspiration must have come from.

I sit down on the remains of a wall, to follow the bird further with my eyes; but it is of a slightly nervous temperament, flying to one branch and then to another, until eventually it obscures itself from my view. Only once it has vanished do I realize I had been holding my breath while watching it, its movements of enormous grace. Now, the silence of the forest is complete. I have the feeling that all this was precisely what I had come to experience, without ever quite knowing what to expect beforehand. And there was the premonition that there must be much more I had not yet even laid eyes upon.

There was more. Slowly, we meandered through gaps in the surrounding walls, past more stupas, crumbling, past *wihans* (as the congregational assembly halls are called) and friezes of Buddhas. The gentler, warmer afternoon light begins to filter through trees of the surrounding jungle, making patterns of chiaroscuro. One feels blessed to be in so divine a place.

Our somewhat detached guide keeps well in the background, barely visible. We are grateful to her for bringing us here but her explanations are irrelevant, seemingly learnt by rote, randomly interpreted; it is just a job to her.

She takes us, nevertheless, to yet another memorable temple, lying inside a bend further down the Yom river. Ancient remains from various ages stand beside a large, active temple with a school attached, as is so often the case. It bustles with happy life.

It is with the greatest pleasure that I return to Thailand for a second visit in 2005, if only for a few days. My desire for temple exploration has not diminished, it has in fact become greater still; and so I thought I would revisit the temple of Lopburi. Like all the other capitals of the past, it is found in the Chao Phrya river basin. In the 10th century Louvo, as it was then called, was the center of the Mon civilization. Later it became a provincial capital of the Khmer Empire, up until Sukothai was established further north. At the time Louvo was famous for being *the* place to study Buddhism, whose teachings the Mon followed.

By the 17th century Lopburi had become the second capital, after Ayutthya—whose realm various European nations already had their eye upon. In 1685 a French embassy, fortified with Jesuit missionaries, arrived; they were received cordially, treated to great pageantry and splendidly entertained. However, when Constantine Phaulkon— the Greek adventurer who had risen to become the most important minister at King Narai's court—started to develop visions of omnipotence, he was done away with as soon as the king died. Lopburi was abandoned and the new king ruled from Ayutthya, and the curiosity and respect for Europeans vanished with the realization of their hunger for power. Their attempts at converting the Siamese to Christianity led to a resurgence of Theravada Buddhism, directed by the new king and his entourage. From then on, only the Chinese traded with Siam. Better the devil one knows....? The Chinese were also, of course, brilliant at sticking to "strictly business".

Being a hound for old capitals, especially if they contained Khmer ruins, I had first driven to Lopburi in 1973. On the way I was unexpectedly elated by the view of endless interlinking ponds, abundant with pink waterlilies, almost entirely covering the surface of the dark water and surrounded by the green of ricefields, stretching to a range of hills on the remote horizon. I realized again, what was behind the inspiration of a piece of silk I had been given: a bright green background covered with large pink waterlilies. At first it had seemed obtrusively bright, but, seen in nature, those overpowering colours produce nothing but awe.

Yet when I returned thirty-two years later, the ponds—or *klongs*, as they are called—had been half transformed into canals. They had nothing but murky brown water in them, were empty of the beauty they used to contain. Here and there, as if to demonstrate my memory had not tricked me, I still found the odd bushel of lilies—but forlorn ones. Fragments of storm drain had also ended up in these klongs, as though waiting to be connected, for someone to put them in place again? Almost everywhere on earth, man over-reaches himself, trying to outwit nature, to improve on it—and destroying it in the process. When I first saw these waterlilies in their ponds, so magnificent in size and number, I hardly believed them to be real. Have people now tired of their fairy tale quality; is it all solely about land ownership? Only the occasional sight of clusters of lotus flowers, white and much wilder-looking, made good this disappointment. They are, after all, the holy flowers of Hinduism and Buddhism. They symbolize the purity of the soul. As we came closer to town they increased in number, but only barely. It seemed the wrong way round. And then came the klongs, strewn with rubbish, yet lined with really rather attractive houses. There is clearly a problem with rubbish collection in Lopburi, as in many fast-growing towns— unlike Bangkok, however, where the streets are faultlessly clean and tidy.

Lopburi is nonetheless well worth seeing—especially once one overcomes the initial shock of dilapidation borne by the two much lesser temples one finds near the railway station, one of them crawling with monkeys. There are several Buddha images inside Prang Sam Yot; but they have been savagely decapitated, every one of them mutilated. The monkeys appear to gloat over the sight. They are more in their rightful place at a nearby open monkey sanctuary, where they look quite playful and, better still, do not crowd one.

But diligence is rewarded. Wat Phra Si Rattana Mahathat is a wonder set amongst the most perfect, broad frangipani trees, whole clusters of them, laden with exquisite waxy blossoms—mostly white but, occasionally, in that lovely lemony yellow, so restrained in its colour, that only frangipanis have. To pick up their fresh blossoms from the grass onto which they have fallen, to inhale their heavenly scent, is one of the great pleasures of the temple enclosures and gardens of this country. It reminded me of Wat Phu on the Mekhong, in Laos; but when I was there the ancient trees were only very slightly in bloom—and still they were beautiful.

There seems to be a Wat Mahathat in every Thai town; it is usually the most important temple. Maha means 'great' in Sanskrit, upon which the Thai language is partly based: as in 'Maharaja' (great king/ruler). They are in fact temples with royal associations; or else they contain relics.

Within the large enclosure of Wat Phra Si Rattana Mahathat lie various religious ruins and, apart from a few workers repairing a Khmer prang, one is alone, surrounded only by the peace of the grassy grounds. The odd statue here, an intricate stucco frieze there; though they are overgrown, the outlines of the classic architectural setup are easy to divine. I am glad the temple is being restored, if only haltingly. But in the heat of a July noon, who could possibly work fast?

Evocative colonial-style houses, made from wood in the last century, stand all around; as if inspired by the remains of the great temple, surrounded by lovingly planted trees.

It is hard to tear oneself away from the enchantment of this spot, so unexpected after the disappointment of the preceding impressions. But the elation stays with one, long after one has left, and—as with every beautiful temple enclosure—so does the vague desire to return one day.

Not surprisingly, King Narai's Palace is not far from here. Its grounds are bounded by enormously thick walls covered in white paint, as they would be at a similar building in India or Burma, and are shaded by huge, gnarly old trees. We drive through the vast elephant gate, with its battlements above. The wooden portal alone, set within the gate of stone, is monstrously large.

Our car, tiny by comparison, enters the well-kept enclosure. It is wonderfully cool below the trees which were planted long ago. This kind of shade must have been the luxury of the day, yet—being a gift of nature—it is so much better than air-conditioning. Seeing the gates, one thinks of the impressive entrance the monarch must have made when arriving on his elephant, seated on a *how-dah*, the rattan and wooden seat which moves with the beast. From long before King Narai's days wars were fought with the king's princes and generals seated on elephants, leading the footfolk. Spears were launched from atop these colossal creatures onto the opposing armies. Small wars though they were, they must have been awesome. The other side, of course, would equally be fronted by elephant-owning leadership. The image must have greatly enforced the idea of the god-king, as at Angkor.

My driver is dismayed: today is Monday, and the palace is closed on Mondays and Tuesdays.

But I cannot just leave. I walk around tentatively, and no-one stops me. As I approach the inner elephant gate, a funny old man appears, asking "where you from" and so on. I have to half-guess what he is saying, but he is friendly; he addresses the uniformed and very proper-looking guard, who has just come through the gate. The two mull things over, and I thought I heard the word "towrai", which means how much, but not directed at me. The aloof guard, with the tidy, sinewy figure of all young Thais, semi-reluctantly lets me in; I wander on into the inner grounds. Apart from the raised temple vihara, which I approach respectfully, all the buildings are closed. Everything appears in perfect order and proportion. They knew how to build for the climate, even hundreds of years ago, long before air-conditioning. The windows are tall but always covered by sloping roofs. Underneath them, huge shutters painted burgundy red punctuate the deep white walls with their imposing symmetry. The abundance of mature trees lowers the temperature deliciously.

Now I really *will* have to come back to Lopburi, to see the palace from the inside. And the museum, which sounds highly promising. But for the time being I am more than happy just wandering about, with no-one distracting me. It is as though they had decided that it was safe to let me and my eyes take in the perfection of their treasure.

Old and new Thai architecture in the provinces is always charming, so human in its proportions, proud but contained. Could it be the influence of Buddhism itself? The ability to restrain oneself, one's desires? As I walk along, a mounting sense of contentment overcomes me; rather than being overwhelmed, I am re-assured by the harmonious interplay between the palace and its grounds, which were restored by King Mongkut.

The thought occurs to me that I must not outstay my, after all, unexpected welcome. I half-heartedly wander back to the gate, which is now firmly padlocked: with an enormous old lock. Hmmm. Will I have a longer stay than I had thought? But no, the guard re-appears and, slowly, opens the gate. Just before I pass through it, I offer a generous tip for the special treatment I have enjoyed. He waves it off, gently, non-committal. How refreshing, after the self-appointed guide at the monkey-infested temple who turned our correct tip over in his hand several times, showing his disapproval. But that is forgotten now. Maybe it was simply a bit of social realism, making the positive parts of the journey stand out more in their significance. Like everywhere else in the world, there are people and there are people. But in my recollection there are many more kind, smiling, gentle people in Thailand than there are anywhere else. This must be due to Buddhism. After all, the inspired leadership of the present king, King Bhumiphol Aduleidet, is deeply grounded in it.

We drive to another temple; I am growing a little less receptive and attentive, I notice. The thumping heat is beginning to tire me after all. Even now the temple's name escapes me. But I do remember the young monk who was inside its hall, who hands me some votive incense sticks and the gold leaf that comes with them. He returns later, after I have lit them in front of the statue of the Buddha and reflected for a while, sitting on the floor, legs to the side, as girls are supposed to; crossing one's legs is for the boys. This is not yoga.

I apply the gold leaf to one of the statues and join the palms of my hands to *wai*, the Thai gesture for giving thanks. After a while, when, slowly and pensively, I begin to leave, the monk, who stands tall and upright at the temple door, hands me two small terracotta votive tablets. We talk a little, and then he welcomes the driver, who is also given a tablet. The driver is surprised, and grateful in his disarmed way. He had been somewhat indifferent before. Perhaps he is a lapsed Buddhist, hardened by his daily exposure to ignorant travellers.

One so often sees people, Europeans, smile at Buddhism in a condescending way. The Thais know this, and they are not offended. They know us to be unaware. And they feel no compulsion to force their knowledge on us. They know that one attains enlightenment only by searching for it oneself. And that there is room for everyone as long as one does not hurt others. It is all so simple, and so obvious. But that very quality makes people distrust Buddhism, in the way, say, the undiscerning consider Mozart's music to be lightweight in its passages of airy sweetness. They may not hear the underlying themes of foreboding, of melancholy, of longing, of avowal, the sum of which makes his genius.

As we drive further north towards Chiengmai in what used to be the Lanna kingdom, which was once invaded by the Burmese but is now a thriving part of Thailand, the presence of the King is everywhere. Banners fly atop entrances to schools and atop all sorts of official enterprises, from agricultural experimentation stations to the army, to seats of learning. His picture is everywhere, slightly otherworldly but kindly as well. And what a distinguished looking King—emanating such dignity, rightfully revered. Amongst many other things, it was his intervention that successfully turned the hill tribes in the Golden Triangle away from opium cultivation—they now happily grow coffee to give them a livelihood, and it is worth their while.

The King of Thailand is not merely a good ruler but a deeply revered monarch, honoured and esteemed by all, regardless of their social origins or their relative level of importance. To say that he is admired seems platitudinous in the context; that is just one of many things that come to mind. There is the thought that a wise God had sent him to be King, which I have heard people say, and which may even be attributed to him himself.

In Europe, crowned heads are often the stuff of derision. The devotion inspired by the King of Thailand would be unthinkable there. Kings and queens must be put down, for no reason other than the fact that they are kings and queens. I see mockery on European faces. In fact, the populace is frequently ill informed by a press that is somewhat limited in outlook, to put it mildly. One almost feels sorry for them. Almost.

The King of Thailand has extended his own dignity to his people. He has been able to, and still is able to, make the culture of his country understood by the world, particularly the Western world, in which, after all, he grew up: first in America and then in Europe. He is a man of infinite humanity, a true Buddhist. When I read his televised New Year's speech after the Tsunami had hit his country, I was greatly moved. I wrote down some of his words: "… that Thais have once again demonstrated the unique harmony and compassion that has preserved the Kingdom for centuries … They are determined to live in peace. They don't leave others in the face of disaster." I can vouch for that, as I have experienced it more than once. And: "They are ready to help others." Also, I quote the Bangkok Post: "The King urged everyone to hold on to harmony and their good hearts, which have been the special elements that have helped save the Kingdom from danger and allowed the nation to live in peace for a long time."

Of course, it all came from India. From there, Buddhism arrived in China overland via Myanmar on the Silk Road, reaching South- and South-East Asia on the Spice Route: that is, through maritime traffic. From Sri Lanka, it travelled along the east coast of India, past Malaya, Sumatra, Java (where the magnificent temple of Borobodur still stands in great glory, nonetheless slightly diminished through its being in a country where there are apparently no more believers), and Bali; and then to Vietnam or Champa, and finally Cambodia, up the Mekhong river. The province of Chen La divided itself into the kingdoms of Laos and Cambodia in the 8th century; King Jayavarman II of Cambodia, who ruled at the end of that century, was supposed to have been Javanese. For this reason one rediscovers Indian styles all over Indo-China, as its art and religion had travelled with the merchants. The easy fusion between Hinduism and Buddhism had also come from India. The Isthmian kingdoms, now southern Thailand and Malaysia, were indianized by the 3rd century. Dvaravati Buddhist ruins, partly inspired by the Gupta art of India, can still be found there. The capital of this Mon kingdom may have been Lopburi, further north. Dvaravati sculpture is often considered the apex of Thai art.

Proof of the fact that Buddhism came from India is clearly to be seen on the reliefs carved into the walls of Angkor Wat and the lintels of other temples. They illustrate the Mahabaratha, the great Indian epic that describes a civil war in India. Additionally, the Ramayana, another Indian epic, is easily identified on these reliefs, as well as on the walls, friezes and statues of most of the other Khmer temples in the region. The participants are the usual protagonists, be they Hanuman the monkey god, Brahma, Sita, Vishnu, Shiva and his son Ganesha, the elephant god, or the ox Nandin or the snake Sesha, on whom Vishnu reclines upon the cosmic ocean.

The great Indian king Ashoka, who lived about 200 years before Christ, turned Buddhism from a folk religion into the guiding light in his life. He had fought many battles, successfully, to extend the empire but eventually he tired of bloodshed and violence and proclaimed himself a Buddhist. He also became a great builder of stupas, to further propagate his faith. Prince Narendraditya, so many centuries later, comes to mind, in a province of the Khmer empire, under whom Phnom Rung was built. King Ashoka of India even sent missionaries to Nakhon Chaisi (which is now Nakhon Pathom, in Thailand—not far from Bangkok, which then did not exist as such) to teach Buddhism. Many stelae still speak of his words, all over India. Gandhi, even though not a Buddhist, was another inheritor of the spiritual concept of non-violence. It was the key to his worldview. I see it as a natural continuation of his cultural and historical background. And he managed to inspire the entire world with his vision, with the purity of it.

It has always seemed to me that the ideals of Buddhism and Christianity are the same. Where Buddhists seek mindfulness and kindness, Christians speak of valuing love above all else. Are not both borne from empathy, and from the attempt to encourage people to act upon this empathy? There is no dogma in Buddhism, though. Tolerance and the neutralization of violence are strongly advocated. Without tolerance the world might soon become an ever-enlarging battlefield; to act on the impulse of revenge usually only leads to more revenge. "War is a disease", as Antoine de Saint-Exupéry said, looking down from above as he was piloting his plane in the then still-lonely skies. So he wrote "Le Petit Prince". Escapist maybe, but what a beautiful book to read to a child. It is now an opera as well, composed by Nikolaus Schapfl and performed to an audience in Salzburg so moved that they shed tears.

The Constitution of the European Union has been drafted under a new dogma, that of not mentioning the undeniable historical fact that the value-system of Europe rests upon the ideals of Christianity. Upon the ideals, not the institution, of the Church. "The Church is but God's establishment on earth", as the British historian Lord Acton said, or so I have been told. Are Europeans growing embarrassed of their Christian origins? In order to respect other religions, as of course one should, one does not have to give up one's own. Good old Marx, creator of a doctrine with religious overtones himself, must be rejoicing (in absentia).

But Buddhism is not just another version of Christianity, far from it. It has its own distinctive character, and much, much to give to this world. Having experienced the birth of my first child in a modern but profoundly Buddhist country (Siam), I can serenely say that it has the capacity of making one happy, if only one lets it. Whether it is a philosophy or a religion. I did not know much about it then, but I loved what it gave to me through the people who believe in it and practice it in their everyday lives.

It is the temples I wanted to write about, though. They are, just like European churches and church music, the product of devotion, not necessarily of devotion to a person, but to an ideal. Only, there is chanting rather than preaching. The best way to approach the rituals of Buddhism as an outsider is just to sit and let one's thoughts wander. And one does reflect, after a while, when one sees people coming in, seeking enlightenment, sometimes with their awed children—they are never despondent. Form is important, too. Shoes are taken off at the entrance; men sit cross-legged, women on one side, with their legs folded on the other. One would not want to disturb the peace of a temple; after all, it is the domain of believers and not of uninitiated visitors. Nonetheless, Buddhist temples are always open and welcoming. What a contrast to Protestant churches, which become cold and forbidding fortresses, firmly locked, once instruction is over.

Another way to approach a temple, old or new, is to slowly walk around it, with the temple on one's right. The walking in itself is meant to lead up to meditation, or at least to a reflective state of mind. The monks in Bhutan do this, touching the prayer wheel as they proceed. Eventually this will produce a kind of trance and one's thoughts, possessive though they may have been, will evaporate.

The sad thing in Bhutan is that, despite all the purity of its religious life and the indeed wonderful settings of its temples, the faithful do not seem to visit them except on festival days. A Bhutanese temple seems to be the exclusive territory of the monks, kind and welcoming to strangers though they are. But the *dzongs*, their temples, are not part of village life. Maybe the small private temple corners people seem to have in their homes are the answer to this. It is quite a contrast to the meditative atmosphere in a Thai temple, where people light their incense and bow to the wisdom of the Buddha. There is such grace to the ritual, such inner grace.

But enough of theory. Let us move on to practice; back in Indochina, that is. There are temples and there are temples. Not all of them inspire, but the older they are, the more they do. The garishness of some of the new ones turns off the visiting purist, but they serve a valuable purpose as the expression of the joie-de-vivre of the villagers, who, after all, support these institutions with the fruits of their labour. Sins committed in concrete are clearly visible all over the world, and why should a modern temple be an exception? The important thing is that the people in a Buddhist community feel the need to give an expression to their beliefs, to support the monks in their work of teaching the children and of being there for all to consult: to direct them and to spread their kindness over them. Their facial expression is, it seems, turned inwards—theirs are not the empty faces one so frequently sees in the street in an exclusively consumerist country.

In a small baroque church high up in the Alps I once unexpectedly heard a Catholic priest cite Buddhism as a source of inspiration and strength. The image on the altar was of Christ lifting his hand in blessing, just like the Buddha, a withdrawn but radiant expression on his face. And a wooden sculpture of Maria holding Jesus, the child, to be adored. In Buddhism as well, men and women are equal in importance, in humanity. Possibly even more so in Buddhism. Which explains the great harmony between the sexes in the countries where life is guided by this wisdom. Still, the fact that Buddhists are non-judgmental can frequently be misleading, as to the uninitiated it can look like indifference.

India. Where Siddharta Gautama found enlightenment under the Bodhi Tree. One such tree is in every Buddhist temple enclosure anywhere, and very much revered. The scene is again and again depicted in paintings and sculptures representing Siddharta's life, such as at Ajanta.

To get to Ajanta, one has to fly to Aurangabad from Mumbai, a short flight into this hilly, stony territory. As always, it is fascinating to observe the changes in the countryside from a plane window. The alternative is ten hours on the road. In Indian traffic.

When one does arrive at Ajanta, and first sees the long line of caves stretching along the winding gorge of the Waghora river, one knows one is in a holy place. The caves contain wall paintings and sculpture, mostly from the Gupta period on, from the 4th to the 6th century. In this era, Indian art is widely considered to have found its finest expression, as it did in literature, drama and music. Temples and palaces of the epoch were known to have been embellished with frescoes. At Ajanta there are also earlier caves from the 1st century on, though they are much more austere and inward-looking. The Gupta influence can still be seen in the wall paintings of Sigirya in Sri Lanka, and even in Bali. The Ajanta caves are esteemed for their paintings, but in fact the sculpture is sublime in the extreme, even though it is never self-conscious, as at the nearby Ellora, built at a later date. Or perhaps because of that. It speaks of ultimate harmony, as achieved by the Enlightened One.

Temple No.2 was the first we entered—and we were overcome with awe. From almost total darkness, the immense figure of a seated Buddha emerged, just as one was slowly getting used to the dim light. His right hand is raised in the *mudra* (as a symbolic hand gesture is called in Sanskrit) of blessing, offering protection. He had been sculpted out of veneration. Seeing this alone could make one into a Buddhist. Human beings are capable of great things, sometimes of the divine, and here it is, for all to see. At least to those receptive to it.

After visiting cave after cave, the impression is intensified over and over again, as more and more exquisite Buddha figures exude ever greater beauty and serenity. The monks who lived here, along the valley of the Tiger River, flowing limpidly below, must indeed have thought they were close to heaven, as they reached an ever finer expression of their thoughts and ideas. They did not find it necessary to add their names to their works, just as artists in medieval Europe did not—the age of self-aggrandizement was still a long way off.

There are few foreign tourists at Ajanta, just some slowly ambulating Indians, women in saris, some of their men holding tiffin carriers, containing lunch for the whole family. With good reason. On the opposite side of the gorge, a small hill presents itself, topped by a pagoda. I never got that far, having spent the day looking at the caves, but I am told it is a perfect place for a picnic. It must be preferable to the restaurant at the entrance, at which we mistakenly ended up. The hill of the pagoda does take three quarters of an hour to walk up to, though, and at an hour when it is very hot ... Had I known, I would have paced myself for the experience. I was also told by the guide that the best time to visit Ajanta is during the monsoon season, when everything is bright and green. To see the water cascading down past the entrances to the caves and then feeding into the river must be a wonderful sight.

The monks who carved these caves out of the overhanging rock and painted them came here during the monsoon themselves, perhaps with other artists, and sanctified them. If there is salvation, one feels close to it while contemplating these expressions of the divine.

There are twenty-seven caves, each more sublime than the next. More still are being painstakingly restored, which is a joy to see. Since Unesco are involved, Buddhist art forms are finally being taken seriously worldwide. Hopefully the philosophy and the religion will be next.

For all potential Buddhist pilgrims, Ajanta's caves are the revelation of something one had imagined subconsciously, without knowing it. The caves are rightly praised for their paintings, but in fact it is their sculpture that reaches the highest lyrical expression. Art historians may not agree, but there *is* also the eye's comprehension of what humaneness represents.

Filing past as if in a trance, visitors—Buddhists or not—are awed by what they see. Theirs is a happy trance, though; they are not laden down with guilt as Christian pilgrims might be. They are easily moved to a smile. There are almost no foreign tourists here, just the odd person here and there. This is wonderfully refreshing, as is the sense of one's acceptance by the Indian visitors, be they local people from the state of Maharashtra or from elsewhere in this vast and diverse country. Before one goes yet further in one's appreciation, it is a feast for the eyes alone to watch the gay, life-affirming colours of the saris, worn with grace and a kind of abandon by all the women, young and old, before the background of the austere, ancient caves. This spectacle unfolds high above the river, which winds its convoluted way through the steep gorge, nonetheless lined with a lush foliage of trees and shrubs which seem to grow on rocks as if by miracle. Again, a sensation of timelessness over-comes one.

My appreciation of the guide, though he is a mine of information, is slightly dimmed by his habit of intermittently spitting. He has a cold, he tells us. The first time I laid eyes on him, expecting a formal greeting and verbal introduction, if not a *namaste*, he spat instead; admittedly, to the side. I was not sure I could interpret this as a gesture of welcome. One tried to ignore it. The funny thing is, he was rather likable despite this irritating habit, which one hoped he might after a while give up. He took a dim view, however, of my mentioning that his torch needed a new battery: which in the darkness of the caves' interiors rather matters, trying as one does to see the somewhat damaged and faded paintings. I admit to watching the other guides' strong torchlight with a degree of envy. Of course, envy: another sin. But here I am, becoming dogmatic like a good European Christian. I should not trivialize this, though, as envy lies at the center of a great many negative emotions.

Ajanta was rediscovered in 1819 by an English cavalryman during a tiger hunt. What a revelation it must have been! Ellora, which is not so far away and which also has a conglomeration of caves, had been found long before as it was on a trade route, and was long known amongst the informed. It is, however, only partly Buddhist. Most of the other cave temples are Hindu and Jain. Certainly the Hindu and Buddhist ones speak of artistic excellence, tradition and know-how, of great skill in the execution of rock carving. Still, the aura of the divine that Ajanta exudes has been trodden down, inexorably, by millions of feet. Well-meaning feet, I am sure, but the presence of too many people destroys so much, even here.

The temples of Ellora were carved after Ajanta had been abandoned, from AD 600 onwards. Had the monks followed the merchants across the sea to Sri Lanka, to Java, to Cambodia and up the Mekhong river valley ... all of which abound with Buddhist temples? Closer by, Sigirya in Sri Lanka possesses cave paintings of this era, which in style and excellence of execution are very close to those at Ajanta (and a great joy to see). Did the monks want to spread their beliefs in the way that Christian missionaries did? Or did they need to flee? Hinduism was in the ascendant then, and maybe the monks were driven away, or at least beginning to feel alienated? Perhaps the abandonment of these caves was unrelated to Buddhism's being spread abroad via the maritime routes, or perhaps not. It would be fascinating to know.

It is not my intention to affront the believers of Hinduism when I compare Ellora to Ajanta—far from it. I am fully aware of the fact that many practices of Buddhism have their roots in Hinduism, and that the two are strongly related. Mahayana Buddhism shows a strong affinity to Hinduism. Even today, Brahmin clergy officiate at the Court of the King of Thailand during important ceremonies like the Ploughing Ceremony or the state funeral given to the Queen Mother, amongst others. As was done a thousand years ago at Angkor. And there we saw the miraculously harmonious co-existence of the two faiths, nourishing one another.

To me, having lived in a Buddhist country, this religion or philosophy of life is more tangible, more welcoming, and easier to comprehend, because it is more abstract. This sounds like a value judgement, which it is not meant to be. A true Buddhist would refrain from making such a judgement. There is, after all, room for all of us.

And, on the other hand, it can be tedious when a writer lacks conviction, fears entrusting his readers with his own thoughts. It is not completely truthful; it can be cowardly. It shows a low opinion of his readers and, perhaps, of humanity. Which does not mean that one needs to be blunt. Form is as important as content; the balance of the two constitutes art. However, it is the art of reflection that makes all the difference, as I am sure a Buddhist would agree.

With the revival of Hinduism in the 7th century AD, Buddhist art in India went into decline, and later works have a somewhat more nebulous appeal. It would be a great mistake, however, not to continue on to Ellora after visiting Ajanta, not necessarily because it is "famous", but because it will deepen one's impression of the Indian aesthetic. Mere rock has become sculpture in the hand of man, sculpture which one can only admire. There are thirty-four caves in Ellora, again in a row, along a gentle precipice. The first twelve are Buddhist, and are earlier than the following ones—from the 7th and 8th century. They are more austere and less elaborate than at Ajanta, but there are some wonderful ones amongst these, too. Above all, an aura of artlessness accompanies one, as one proceeds from one cave to the next. Cave 12, a monastery, is particularly inspirational and impressive, if one does not miss the upper hall, inundated as it is with columns and exquisite sculptures of Boddhisatvas and Buddhas. Boddhisatvas are potentially heavenly creatures who stay on earth to help others, and they are always beautiful and wise-looking. One does hope they do not only exist in stone.

The important Cave 10 is thought to have been the hostel of a monastery, full of carvings, including one of the Buddha seated under the Bodhi tree in preaching mudra.

The sculptures of the sixteen Hindu caves are breathtaking, the central Kailasha shrine, carved with celestial figures, being the masterwork. Worshippers file past the lingam and other symbols as if in a dreamlike trance. Here we again come across the Ramayana and Mahabaratha epics, battle scenes, as well as a touching, affectionate rendition of the bull Nandi. He looks like a baby bull, childlike. He is obviously much esteemed, and devotees file past him, too. Kailasha is the Himalayan mountain home of Shiva and his divine consort Parvati. It is well guarded by imposing elephants; at times the mountain is even held up by them. In ancient

Indian tradition, the elephant is held to be the wisest of all animals.

The thronging masses steer one along, nevertheless, and it becomes hard to concentrate in depth while one is occasionally wiped out of the way. But it is good to see the Indians value their own culture so highly, so happily immersed in it as they are within their own country. India has so much to give to humanity, too much to grasp for one coming from another culture.

One could spend all one's life visiting Buddhist temples, there are so many. There were the land trade routes and the sea trade routes, and the religious conviction and the art inspired by it arrived on both of them. It started with Pollonaruwa and Anuradhapura in Sri Lanka, where Buddhism was reformed; and from where Sinhalese Buddhism traveled, to the exquisite Pagan in Burma, which used to contain three thousand temples and is encircled by the Irawaddy river. It moved on past the Suwannaphuma and Dvaravati kingdoms in the Chao Phrya river basin, and past small settlements in the Thai isthmus, down to Java, with Borobodur (rediscovered by Raffles, but only as an edifice). And, with smaller temples en route, it moved to Cambodia too, with provinces stretching as far as Burma, such as the Mun River civilization, as one travels up the Mekhong river. This is where Theravada Buddhism, as created under the Indian King Ashoka and later reformed in Ceylon, spread.

It seems that all major sacred sites of Buddhism are to be found in a divine, earthly setting. Even

Taxila, in present-day Pakistan, has an aura of the wondrous, though not a single wall is standing any more to remind one of the illustrious past of Greco-Buddhist art in the Gandharan province. I am not even mentioning the more austere temples of Northern Asia—Bhutan's are superb, though not as accessible to eye and body as those in the South. Mahayana Buddhism, as practiced in northern Asia, is the more austere form, whereas the Theravada form is the more adaptable to modern life. Which I think is its strength, a true strength which it gives back to those who observe it in a modern country like Thailand. And it works. I have come across more acts of grace and kindness in Thailand, where I lived for far too few years, than anywhere else in the world. Given out of a spirit of gentleness and generosity. Not just gentleness in physical action, but in thought itself. The value of gentleness, and with it the generosity of empathy, represent the opposite of the aggressive

enforcing of one's will, regardless of how destructive this may be.

Looking down from the plane, watching the
graceful curve of the Chao Phraya river carrying
its abundant, fast-flowing water, lined by wats
and by stupas here, there and everywhere, I long
to be re-united with the land of a thousand elephants, as Laos used to be called—and Siam
should have been even more so. The name may
have become a cliché, but it told the truth, it even
understated it. It would be sad to be cynical and
all-knowing about Asia: the dismissiveness of the
"old hands", the expatriates, which was despicable

to me from the start. It does not give its people a chance.

Bangkok is changing at an alarming rate, as are most big cities in the world, yet somehow here it hurts even more. The charming small *sois*, lanes coming off wide roads, with their grassy edges and their ambulant street vendors, bearing carts of food and drink and always with time for a chat, have made room for more asphalt, more traffic and many more larger, higher buildings. Gardens are increasingly squeezed into the shadow of high rises. The dreamy quality of the slow pace of everyday life is being eaten up by the profit motive, even here.

One thing, though, has remained the same—the phenomenon of the soi dogs. My old friend Toto is one of them. He used to live contentedly in a house, but he was exiled for the crime of digging up the perfectly kept lawn, and now he is a proper soi dog. He has learnt to defend himself. What a fighter he has become! As always, they are a wild bunch, these canines, sunning themselves during the day, heads with pensive, darkly ringed eyes resting on dirty yellow paws, looking on accusingly. Or else they just wander about, looking decidedly busy. At night, however, the drama begins, as mere humans try to sleep. The dogs fight an ugly fight for male sexual supremacy. There is a lot of screeching and appalled barking as if to demonstrate orally the cruelty of nature, while the female dogs cower. One must feel sorry for the bitches, hard though it is to admire them. But *they* end up having the young, endlessly, while the aggressive males just get lost, ready for the next fight.

The other cacophony that reminds me of my first years in Bangkok is that of the buses speeding along the empty roads of the night. And speed they do: one can hear the roar from miles away. There is something threateningly alien, and violent, about the unstoppable brute force of this sound, even in one's memory.

Not everything about modernity is regretful, even I must admit. The new net of flyovers takes the longer-distance traffic away from the smaller local roads. Getting to the airport is quick now. And then there remains the famed Ho Chi Minh Trail of this city, known to residents only, and so called in the quirky Thai sense of irreverence. It is an endlessly winding assemblage of tiny, interlinking roads which snake through the sois, where people actually live. The Trail enables one to get about without ever coming into the often clogged main artery of the Sukhumvit Road. And the name reveals a hidden admiration for the clandestine genius of the oppressed, if not exactly for the

Vietcong. And, of course, it divulges their delight in outwitting the sanctimonious Americans, possessed by a feeling of moral and cultural superiority as they were.

Which brings me to the subject of some of the supposedly enlightened, and indeed acclaimed, writers of today. Suddenly, in the middle of the churning river, sitting in a long-tail boat speeding past Wat Arun, the exquisite Temple of Dawn—which rises almost opposite the equally inspiring 16th century Wat Pho—suddenly I am struck by what cultural aggression and ignorance can do. That a European, a relatively educated European, could view this country with the disdain and neo-colonial condescension of Michel Houellebecq in *Plateforme*, is profoundly disillusioning and saddening. When one thinks that the Europeans might have learnt something from past errors, to hear a youngish man, who has all the choices, descend into a voyeuristic exploitation of another culture, one is overcome with nausea. It puts him in the same category as Paul Theroux, whose words from *The Great Railway Bazaar*—"Bangkok smells of sex"—gives away entirely what he had come to see; while taking the morally high tone, which grates even more.

When I first arrived in Thailand in 1973, the men and women of the people, and the women of the upper classes, were proud to wear sarongs at parties. They all, without exception, looked superb with their command of their slender, wiry bodies within this piece of cloth—because this is all it is, albeit tied in an artful, body-conscious way. The languorous gait of these creatures clad in sarongs was one of the feasts for European eyes, as one realized at the same time that the natural grace of the Asian body, accentuated by slender hips, was totally beyond the realms of possibility for a European—the comparison making Europeans feel like elephants. Now the Thais wear jeans, which must be far too hot for the exceptional heat and humidity of this near-equatorial climate. And they do not suit the Asian figure nearly as much; they look best on lanky people with extra-long legs. I know there must be a desire to be like everyone else in the world, and this is very democratic. But Asian grace vanishes in such unsuitable and unimaginative clothes. But this may be beside the point: Asians might see it differently.

Will saris be next to go, I wonder? I hate to think of it. The spectacle of Indian women everywhere in their deliciously flowing saris exudes joie-de-vivre, even in places such as London. And the colours … Many of the richer young Indian women already wear Western clothes. These things are the same everywhere. The clothes from the supposedly more developed West are mostly dull, they need re-thinking, re-inventing all the time, to keep the industry going.

There used to be street markets all over Thailand: busy, colourful places. As the large supermarket chains grow, though, such markets are in danger of disappearing. To be consumerist is definitely not part of Buddhist thinking, yet people cannot resist the modernisation of their everyday lives. To go to a supermarket one needs a car; one is tempted into buying things one does not need; one is alienated from the unfortunate person at the checkout. In America now, farmers' markets try to regain the lost territory of food shopping in a friendly atmosphere: chatting with the vendor, the fun of choosing appetizing things. In a supermarket the same act becomes a tiresome burden. And people go home to eat a mountain of old food, cleverly preserved to the risk of their health. And forever try to keep their weight down, which is really an artificial thing to have to do.

I was poignantly reminded of this by the work of the contemporary Thai artist Manit. His invention is Pink Man, which sounds more facile than it is. Pink Man is indeed pink all over. He wears a suit, trying to cover up his indulgences in fast food. He slouches, when the Thais of old had the most admirable comportment, because, I was told, they slept on the floor. They were thin, yet muscly. Pink Man holds onto a pathetic pink supermarket trolley (or does the trolley hold onto him?) He wears pink shoes, even. And he most definitely does not smile. Pink Man stands in the

ricefields and temple enclosures of Bali, surrounded by the arts of many centuries, surrounded by a wisdom he has catapulted himself
out of. He stands amidst half-finished construction projects, looking lost …

But Pink Man does not harm anyone, only himself. Yet many pink men would. It is to the credit
of the Thai mentality that even this criticism of
modern life has a (totally unsentimental) affection for the condition of man. It is ridiculous, it is
tragic, and it is human. Errare humanum est.

The photographs of Manit's Pink Man will be
exhibited in Berlin's "House of the Cultures of
the World", a museum with a suitably long name,
in the German tradition. The exhibition brings
contemporary art from South East Asia to
Europe, with music and talks. Since most countries of South East Asia have a Buddhist past as

well as, in many cases, a Buddhist present, it will be fascinating to those open to the subject. Manit's work is not nearly as slick and superficial as it looks at first glance. Value judgements are not the answer.

Nevertheless, nostalgia for a vanishing way of life in Asia slowly established itself amongst some of the long-term residents from the West. Occasionally purely for the sake of regaining old glories, but only occasionally. The nostalgia is now being felt in South East Asia by a local population with a gathered cultural awareness. By those who have tasted the supposedly superior ways of the West.

Of course, modern life has much to recommend itself. I myself would no longer be alive had it not been for modern drugs. Yet the wisdom of the old culture must not be lost. The very same is true of old Europe. But that would be another book.

The word 'democratic' has a purpose, but it is all too often used as a cover-up, as an excuse for low standards. The alienation of modern life also brings the veneration of trash culture. It appears to become the accepted way to live by ever more people. I do not know how democratic this is, although it is within reach of all but those who are most appalled by it. Poor humanity. The noble in man seems to have lost its desire to be passed on, to guard what is valuable and inspirational. In a world brimming with bullies and ogresses, with noise pollution and the ongoing brutalization of the countryside, both visually and chemically, only the banal continues to be celebrated.

A European constitution has been proposed in which Christianity is supposed to be irrelevant. Living in Southern Europe as I do, I find this ludicrous. The majority of villages, as well as the people themselves, have the name of a saint; the most beautiful building in most communities is the church. The works of art of the past, from architecture to sculpture, painting and music, were so often created in the spirit of God. One may not believe in Christianity, but to deny its existence is like telling the Dalai Lama that there is no Buddhism. The Church may have been cruel and unjust in the past, and may be so even now occasionally, but it is in the end no more than the Establishment of God on Earth. The artists who created sublime works in the name of their God were thinking of their faith, rather than power politics. So much so that in the Middle Ages and up to the Renaissance they did not even sign their names, they were happily anonymous.

Much like those who added their works to Hindu and Buddhist temples. They believed in the sublime, the enlightened. The trash culture of those days has happily vanished, as trash cultures always do. A work of art is not bound to any particular age. Which is why one can value so many works of art from so many epochs, whichever one loves most.

The influence of European aesthetics in Thai art is sometimes considered to be an aberration. This ignores that the strength of Siam has always been to be non-confrontational, not in the sense of ignoring outside influences but, on the contrary, in the sense of absorbing them to strengthen her own position. There is a kind of tender affection in some adoptions of European painting techniques, as though the painters were feeling further inspired. They were reaching out, desiring to be part of a larger world, as opposed to being inward-looking and self-congratulatory.

River of the Lords of Life, flowing from the rice-rich Central Plains down through Bangkok into the Gulf of Siam.

But let me return to the year I reluctantly left Angkor. I arrived back at my friends' house in Bangkok to find it empty, even though I knew they were expecting me. Eventually, one of the maids emerged, then another, to say that their employers had gone out. Then they mumbled something about "airbus". Shamefully, I realized yet again, my Thai vocabulary and comprehension were not up to understanding what they were saying. The word "airbus" came up several times more, obviously meant to convey a meaning in some obscure way. They seemed confused, upset even, which is so rare in this country of the composed. Suddenly I got it—there had been a plane crash. Was it an airbus? In the South, on one of the islands … I had read about it in the English-language Cambodian paper, just a short notice in a very short paper. But I knew that Spha and Manuela were in Bangkok, so why.…

Luckily, they arrived back soon after I had become confused. Their faces were ashen. Slowly, Spha got out of the car and, instead of the usual welcoming noises and gestures, he said, seeing the non-comprehending expression on my face, "Mark is dead. He was on the Airbus".

The realization of the tragedy overcame me fast, re-enforced by the pained faces of my friends. "I am the executor of his will. We've just seen the lawyer."

Mark Graham was dead. A man whom we had perhaps never taken quite seriously enough, hugely irreverent creature that he was. Mark, of the stinging tongue. Dogmatic, delightful, Mark of the vivid eyes and untamable hair and the warm, embracing manner that surfaced only when one least expected it, when one thought one had had enough of him for quite a while. Mark, who after ten or so bad years, after his wife had left, was finally re-emerging as the generous-spirited, all-embracing man that he had been all along. Mark, whom we were all so fond of, as we now realized. A hammer-blow. We had admired him for his erudition, and ultimately for his human warmth (when it had been forthcoming). Mark, who had still had so much in front of him, even now. Our friend. I did not even know that the very next day a long leader was to appear in the Bangkok Post, written by him, about the disappearance of the tiger in Thailand. On the need to protect the animal:".... tigers, almost extinct in Siam, too," as he wrote. I had no idea that he, of all people, cared, and so openly. Nor did I know about his interest in conservation. Nor that he wrote so well, without a trace of cynicism. I now realized that I did not possess a single one of his, as it turned out, several books, since I never knew he had written them. "He never talked about what really interested him," said Spha, with a shrug and a slight shake of the head.

We were standing by the side of the road next to their four-wheel drive brought back from America. The small vanities and practicalities of life seemed so utterly irrelevant now, so pointless. A void had opened in front of us.

An overall void of feeling, even between all of us. It took a while for the shock to sink in. Mark's children? Teddy said he was looking after them. The huge responsibility.

Slowly and dejectedly, we wandered into the house. A part of our lives had been ended, abruptly and totally unexpectedly. That this should happen to Mark, who had had no sense of the tragic, to him of all people. He had knowingly done so many dangerous things in his life, only then to die in a plane crash. A crash in which two thirds of the passengers had survived—so why not he? It turned out that the front of the plane had hit the ground, a swamp, and those sitting in front had been squashed. Those at the back had walked off the site.

After the elation of Angkor one's existence had become totally sober. We were dazed, all of us.

Nevertheless, the wisdom of practicing Buddhists was there to comfort us.

Mark's funeral was a great experience for me, quite apart from the fact that it was *his*. Although it did feel as though he had invited me.

He began life as a Christian, and he died a
Buddhist. No-one knew this until it surfaced
when his will was read. In it, he had said clearly
that he wanted a Buddhist funeral, which extends
over a whole week, up to the last moment of cre-
mation. Every night the mourners congregate at
the temple, for a full week.

We drove to Wat Mongkut, where the rites were
held, on the way to the Grand Palace complex. It
was a magical night: there were lights, garlands of
flowers, wonderfully illuminated wide boule-
vards, and one recognised yet again, almost in
shock, how beautiful the old part of Bangkok is. I
had often marvelled at it, but it had never
appeared quite as magnificent as on this night.
"The King's birthday", explained Spha laconi-
cally, perhaps not wanting to talk. The dreamlike
effect of the illumination was wonderful to me; it
heightened the emotion of what we were going

through. It also made me think of a Balinese funeral, a joyous feast. Bali, of course, is Hindu. And long may it stay so.

The temple was exquisite. One approached through topiary which had been there for centuries, painstakingly tailored still, until one finally arrived at the doors, almost large enough for an elephant. They tapered towards the top, in the Rattanakosin style of the 19th century, when Bangkok had just been established as the capital of Siam. The doors were heavy. Thick black lacquer fortified them further, on top of which deliciously fine and delicate gold paintings told the story of the Ramayana symbols as absorbed in Siamese religious history. In the artificial light these paintings in chiselled gold stood out even more than they would have done in the unforgivingly fierce sunlight of the day. They were full of grace. The entrance to the Wat was certainly not for the faint of heart: it exuded the pride of a great culture.

Inside, the maze of courtyards and interlinking buildings of a sprawling monastic complex. Never having been here before, I was led through them like a lamb.

Finally we arrived at the more intimate hall where the ceremony was taking place. *There* were the monks on a dais, cross-legged and, as always, clad in their saffron robes. They were chanting, a monotonous chanting, but not unpleasant to the ear. After a while it seemed to make more sense—musical sense—although I could not follow the words. Many words were repeated, which led to a comforting lull, the comfort we needed.

Mark's children, fully grown but, oh so sad. One forlorn, with immensely wide eyes, one consisting only of tears. And his brothers, sturdy men from England and Italy; his parents were ill and unable to travel. They had initially disapproved of his living in Thailand, but had eventually come to terms with it. And now …

His Thai wife, who had left him, was there, too. They had, despite it all, managed to remain friends.

And all the other friends, so many of them. I had not seen them for many, many years. With every face a new image came back. I was amazed at how many friends we had had in common. If I had stayed on in Thailand (as, I realized the day I left, I would love to have done), some of these people would have been my friends still. But with the distances of continents between us, only those who travelled back and forth still were. Which made it twice as touching when they remembered one.

We sat silently. Some people arrived, some left, all noiselessly. Rather like in a Catholic church. But also, here and there, quietly whispered conversations; not conspiratorial, but putting their thoughts into words to let the others know. There was affection for the dead man in all of this, which spread through the congregation; a huge affection. As though everyone had always seen through him, even in his rebellious or more unbearable moments.

Then a ceremony was performed through which a mourner could, with the help of physical means, confide his thoughts to the dead person. The monks had extended a long, sacred cotton thread which was in some way attached to the body, and to the lustral water. Blessed water. By holding onto the other end of the thread, one's thoughts would be channelled towards the deceased. It sounds ridiculous and absurdly thought-up, but in fact it is not. One took the thread and let one's thoughts travel to Mark. The strange thing was that one really felt that one could communicate with him. That he would receive one's thoughts.

One by one, the Buddhist members of the congregation were enacting this, solemnly. When it came to Manuela's turn, she declined. She had often said that she was not religious. But I encouraged her, saying that I was going to do it, and then we, too, went forward to perform the ritual. What had held me back at first was the fear of making a fool of myself, being uninitiated. But then I knew that goodwill, however clumsy, will communicate itself, and will be recognized. So I went down on my knees in front of everyone. There was no hope of being remotely as dignified as the Thais were when doing this. I took the thread. And it was wonderfully healing to have had a chance to say, silently, some of the words that one had never had the courage to say to him in his lifetime. It was not just for him, it was for us as well.

Another year, and again I walk into the old structure of a Thai house which Spha and Manuela had brought down from the country to put up their visiting friends. I walk past the languid pool and then past the muddy pond, where fish far too large for its size had emerged, quite naturally. I duck, so as not to hit my head on the wooden embellishments, knowing that some of my taller predecessors had shed blood when they forgot to accommodate the curves of old Thai buildings—banging their heads, sending them flying and sprawling. The path winds through bamboo in large, healthy green clusters, barely swaying in an imperceptible breeze. Orchids in hanging pots dangle along the way, their untidy roots reminding one of the great disorder of the jungle.

Inside, carefully cut and arranged orchids in Bencharong pots greet one, before one catches sight of an exquisite woven silk bedspread, of hardly decipherable design. The interior as well as the exterior of this house are all wood: dark and comforting after coming in from the searing sunlight. To walk, barefoot, on these beautiful teak floors is always one of the first pleasures I notice. It seems unfair that my generous friends who own all this should have to sleep in their modern house while I enjoy the aesthetics of old Siam. I suppose on a permanent basis convenience and space are more important than authenticity and a sentimental attachment to the past.

Without which nothing would exist. The pretty jasmine garlands which are used on objects, decorative or not, as well as on Buddha statues, spirit houses holding guard, and people alike—it must take so long to string them. The result is of such perfection that now one even sees plastic replicas. One is moved to disdain at this—but then one notices the culture of detachment around one, the absence of value judgements, which make one admire this country so much in the first place. There is no perfect place on earth, as the banal truth has it—but the Thais extend tolerance well beyond the horizon of thought.

I lie down on the bed, breathing in the atmosphere of being well cared for—more than just being looked after. Enveloped by tranquility, one's desire for peace fully protected; one's need for it is, in fact, expected. The consciousness of well-being in this cultivated Thai family house is one of the greatest pleasures on earth.

In whichever way, each day should be a celebration of life. My own thought now, too, but brought on by Buddhist teaching in the beginning.

SELECTIVE SUGGESTED READING

Michael D. Coe : Angkor and the Khmer civilization (Thames & Hudson, London 2003)

Michael Freeman : Khmer temples in Thailand and Laos (River Books, Bangkok 1996)

Thich Nhat Hanh : The Miracle of Mindfulness (Beacon Press, Boston 1987)
Hermann Hesse : Siddharta

Charles Higham : The Civilization of Angkor (Phoenix, London 2001)

Sumet Jumsai : Naga (Chalermnit Press and DD Books, Bangkok 1997)

W. Somerset Maugham : The Gentleman in the Parlour

Hugo Munsterberg : Art of India and Southeast Asia (Harry N. Abrams, New York 1970)

Smitthi Siribadhra, Elizabeth Moore : Palaces of the Gods (River Books, Bangkok 1992)

SOME WORDS USED IN THE TEXT

APSARA   Celestial nymph, who dances and enlightens, and often adorns Khmer temples

BARAY   Reservoir   (Sanskrit)

BAS-RELIEF   Low relief sculpted into the stone

BRAHMA   The Creator, born from Vishnu's navel. Brahma, Vishnu and Shiva form the Trimurti (trinity).

CHEDI   Freestanding reliquary shrine in the form of a spire, rounded towards the ground.

GANESHA The elephant god, son of Shiva

GUPTA In this period of Indian history the arts flourished enormously and the Buddhist university of Nalanda was created in AD 5. Dvaravati art in central Thailand (6th–11th century) was influenced by Gupta art forms. (see Mon)

GURU Brahmin spiritual guide

HANUMAN   Monkey general, from the Ramayana

KHMER Ancient kingdom, now Cambodia

KHMER ROUGE Communist-inspired occupational force of Cambodians, who took over the country at the end of the Vietnam war, and managed to decimate their own people by one quarter.

LINGA   Much revered Hindu symbols of male and

YONI   female fertility.

LINTEL   Rectangular stone block across the top of a door, carved

LON NOL   Cambodian government troops

MAHABHARATA   Eminent Indian epic of feud between dynasties—much depicted in Indian and Khmer temple carvings

MAHOUT   Elephant driver, directing the elephant from above his neck

MANDAPA   Antechamber at the entrance to a temple

MON   Buddhist people inhabiting parts of southeast Burma and central Thailand, where they created the Dvaravati culture, from early 6th century

MOUNT MERU   Symbolic mountain home of the gods, the Himalayas

MUDRA   Symbolic hand gesture of the Buddha or a Hindu deity

NAGA   (Sanskrit)   Multi-headed water serpent, which protected the Buddha

NAMASTE   Indian greeting, much like the Thai "Wai", during which the palms of the hands are joint and raised in greeting. Means "bowing to you" in Hindi, from Sanskrit.

NANDIN   The sacred bull on which Shiva appeared

ORIENTAL   Fabled hotel on the Chao Phraya River flowing through Bangkok, which has attracted writers for a century and continues to do so (including this one).

PATHET LAO   Communist faction, still governing Laos, formed during Vietnam War

PEDIMENT   Upper part of the front of a building, above an entrance, carved

PRANG   Tower above a Khmer temple

PRASAT   Tower of a sanctuary as in southern India. And: temple, palace (from Sanskrit, the

Indian language used by the Khmer ruling class; political and religious.)

RAMAYANA   (or Ramakien in Thai)   Hindu epic, also narrated in dance form to this day, in which Rama tries to regain his wife Sita, who had been abducted by the demon king Ravana.

SANSKRIT   Ancient Indian language and script of scholarship and religion, also used by priests and rulers in the Khmer empire

SHIVA   Hindu god of destruction and rebirth

SIDDHARTA   Buddha, the Enlightened One

SITA   Wife of Rama (see Ramayana)

SOI (Thai) Small residential lane away from major traffic flow

STELA Freestanding stone incised and inscribed upon

STUPA Dome-shaped Buddhist shrine (can also be chedi)

UMA Shiva's consort, daughter of the Himalayas

VIHARA (Sanskrit) Large inner sanctum and congregation hall

VIHARN (Thai) of a

VIHEAR (Khmer) Buddhist monastery

VISHNU   Hindu god of compassion and preservation

WAI (see Namaste)   greeting, prayer and thank you gesture in Siam

WAT   Buddhist temple in Thailand, Cambodia and Laos

978-0-595-42654-6
0-595-42654-9

Printed in the United Kingdom
by Lightning Source UK Ltd.
118510UK00002B/73-300